# Cultural Misunderstandings

**RAYMONDE CARROLL**

# Cultural
# Misunderstandings

## THE FRENCH-AMERICAN EXPERIENCE

Translated by Carol Volk

**THE UNIVERSITY OF CHICAGO PRESS**
Chicago and London

RAYMONDE CARROLL was born in Tunisia, educated in France and the United States, and now teaches at Oberlin College. She has published a book of legends from Micronesia, *Nukuoro Stories*, collected while she lived for three years on a Pacific atoll.

Originally published as *Evidences invisibles*,
© Editions du Seuil, 1987.
The University of Chicago Press, Chicago 60637
The University of Chicago Press, Ltd., London
© 1988 by The University of Chicago
All rights reserved. Published 1988
Printed in the United States of America
97 96 95 94 93 92 91 90 89          5432

Library of Congress Cataloging-in-Publication Data

Carroll, Raymonde.
    Cultural misunderstandings : the French-American experience /
Raymonde Carroll ; translated by Carol Volk.
        p.   cm.
    ISBN 0-226-09497-9
    1. United States—Relations—France.   2. France—Relations—United
States.   3. Americans—Communication.   4. French—Communication.
5. Intercultural communication.   I. Title.
E183.8.F8C26 1988
303.4'8273'044—dc19                                          88-12098
                                                                  CIP

For all interculturals

*Stutzker*

13⁶¹

Sept. 90

81451

# Contents

# Preface

My studies in anthropology had not entirely prepared me. A few hours after our arrival on Nukuoro, an atoll in the Pacific where we were to do three years of field research, we were settled in the best house on the island, the house of wood and corrugated iron that belonged to the chief. The next morning, awakened early by a sense of the unfamiliar, I discovered that the chief had slept on the verandah floor ("to protect our possessions," he told me); he had prepared coffee for us and had washed our baby's diapers. The anthropologist in me did not express astonishment, I only thanked him for his kindness. The next morning, the same scenario; the following day as well. No matter how much I protested, he continued to wash the diapers, despite the evident surprise of the other Nukuoro. He seemed, moreover, to want to draw attention to this uncommon activity, since he had begun to do this washing in the middle of the day, in full view of everyone in the village.

Then the chief, who spoke English fluently, asked me, with a stern look, if I had clipped my baby's fingernails. I thereupon performed this task, under his attentive gaze. He began to watch my every move, but only insofar as it concerned the baby. As our daughter, according to the Nukuoro, was the first white baby that most of them had ever seen or touched, she was a celebrity, and I was not overly surprised by the extraordinary attention the chief lavished upon her. But the fifth day, as I was giving my daughter some baby food under the same watchful eyes, the chief calmly announced that he had decided, actually upon our arrival, that he would take her in adoption, and that he felt the time had come to tell me.

From something theoretical and exciting, anthropology abruptly became something difficult to live. That day, I understood the urgency and distress of certain intercultural exchanges.

In this case, however, the difficulty was not insurmountable: the situation was delicate, but the misunderstanding was at least visible, recognizable, apparent; it was therefore only a matter of finding an adequate response, which I did, of course, once the first moment of panic had passed.

I later discovered how much greater were the consequences of those cultural misunderstandings that only analysis can bring to light. My fieldwork has not stopped since. It has, in fact, invaded—and pervaded—my daily life.

The present work might be presumptuous if it were not, first of all, a look at myself, a "reading of self." It is the product of a polycultural childhood and youth, of an intercultural marriage, of anthropological studies and research, of teaching my language and literature in a foreign country, of hetero- and homocultural friendships in a foreign country. Cultural analysis has allowed me to domesticate this constantly reinforced schizophrenia, to accept it fully, and, finally, to savor its richness and creativeness.

I married an American, an anthropologist by trade. My culture, his culture, intercultural misunderstandings, the comedy of errors, the pain of incomprehensible snags, the constantly renewed awareness of deep and fascinating differences, the interpretations, theories, and impassioned and passionately interesting discussions have, for over twenty years, been everyday occurrences.

My teaching, in several American universities, has drawn its form and perspective from a leitmotiv in the commentary of my students when faced with any type of French text (whether cultural, literary, linguistic, cinematographic, or musical): "I find it sort of weird," or else "It was very bizarre," and similar variations on this theme. In order to make them understand such a text, in order to make them love it, I first had to understand the strageness of what I had found beautiful and had never had to question, to subject it to a new type of analysis, a cultural analysis.

Experiences of this kind led me to do fieldwork in France and in the United States, just as I had done for three years on Nukuoro, the Polynesian atoll in Micronesia to which I alluded earlier: field research, with all the customary interviews, tape recordings, observations, and field notes.

Over the past ten summers, I interviewed informants in Normandy, Paris (and environs), La Rochelle, Tours, the Tarn region (in particular in one very small village), and the Midi. I interviewed French people of all sorts, from a famous writer to a ninety-year-old former waitress. They all granted interviews with the same grace. In the United States, I saw reflections of my behavior in that of other French people, whom I met in large numbers. French people of all sorts: longtime residents, some adapted, some unadaptable, some right off the boat, some celebrities on tour, some first-time visitors, some habitual visitors; people of all ages, some passing through, some who knew it all and some who were curious, some who were enthusiastic and some who were blasé . . . French men and French women. Some irritated me, some (at times) embarrassed me. But they all enriched me with their (conscious or unconscious) testimonies; they all gave me the gift of their presence—an inexhaustible source of "living texts." I would like to thank them for that here.

As for Americans, they have been all around me for more than twenty years, always present, since I live in their country. They too have been constantly interviewed, recorded, observed. With them too I have chatted, talked seriously, laughed, cried, loved, reflected—shared everything. I thank them all here too.

On both sides, the same remarks about the other culture were repeated with a compelling regularity which called for attention. Sometimes it seemed as if the misunderstandings were so ingrained that the Americans and the French would never be able to understand each other. Yet on both sides I found the same desire to understand the other, as was apparent in the interest shown whenever I proposed my interpretations. In fact, I began writing this book because those with whom I shared my analyses constantly encouraged me to do so, assuring me that these analyses had been useful to them and would be for others. I was struck repeatedly by the frequency of intercultural misunderstandings, principally in our close interpersonal relationships, by the number of wounds, deep and superficial, that were essentially due to the profound differences in our cultural premises.

I focused on these misunderstandings between the French and Americans. What interests me here is not to compare "American culture" to "French culture," which is an immense, if not impossible, task, but to identify areas of contact, meeting points between the two cultures where there is, so to speak, a hitch; that is to say, I have tried to identify the context in which cultural misunderstandings can arise. Of course, a misunderstanding is not necessarily going to arise each time the setting is right. But it is important to be able to recognize those areas in which cultural misunderstandings can easily occur and can cause pain, because they are not recognized as cultural—as owing to differences in cultural presuppositions of which we are unaware, to implicit ideas we harbor within ourselves unknowingly, to the way we see the world, one which was learned but which seems to us "natural" or "evident," or which appears to "go without saying." I will return to this matter in the introductory chapter.

Clearly, if I maintain that our interpersonal relationships are informed by our cultural expectations, then the same is true of the logic that informs my analyses, which, in turn, become cultural texts susceptible of analysis. Indeed, it is not by accident that certain people feel the need to analyze certain things (like cultural misunderstandings) while others do not.

In conclusion, I would like to thank those who have helped me in so many ways during the research for, and the writing of, this book. The fact that I am expressing my gratitude in the traditional form in no way diminishes its sincerity. We may write in solitude, but no one writes alone.

I would like to thank sincerely all those who had the patience and kindness to allow themselves to be interviewed. Their identities have, of course, been carefully disguised. If we see ourselves in them, it is because we are them as much as ourselves.

I thank Oberlin College for having supported my research, and the Foundation Franco-Américaine, in Paris, for having given me access to their files. Finally, I thank my many colleagues, my students, my friends, and my family, on both sides of the Atlantic, for having ceaselessly listened and read, for having encouraged, supported, and criticized me. For the time they devoted to my manuscript, I thank Patricia Baudoin, Pierre Bourdieu, Tama Carroll, Ross Chambers, Isdey Cohen, Dolly Esdraffo, Clifford Geertz, Rémo Guidiéri, Bernadette Hogan, Magdeleine Hours, Simone Kelman, Jacqueline Leiner, Marie-Thérèse Neil, Michel Pierssens, Claudine Raynaud, Francine Roure, Robert Soucy, Pierre Tabatoni, Alexandra Tcherepennikova, Viviane Vareilles, and Laurence Wylie. Last but not least, I thank Vern Carroll, without whom I might never have discovered anthropology, and without whom I would probably never have discovered the potential contribution of cultural analysis to actual intercultural experience.

# Introduction

In the following series of essays I have attempted to discover the sources of some frequent cultural misunderstandings which occur between the French and Americans in several important areas of interpersonal relationships. My intention is to provide a point of departure, to indicate a pathway for those who would like to understand what separates us. This study is far from exhaustive. By its very nature, in fact, this type of study can never be complete. Nothing illustrates this fact better, in my opinion, than the story that Clifford Geertz relates in his book, *The Interpretation of Cultures:*

> There is an Indian story—at least I heard it as an Indian story—about an Englishman who, having been told that the world rested on a platform which rested on the back of an elephant which rested in turn on the back of a turtle, asked (perhaps he was an ethnographer; it is the way they behave), What did the turtle rest on? Another turtle. And that turtle? "Ah, Sahib, after that it is turtles all the way down."

This is indeed the way cultural analysis presents itself. The more one does, the more there is to do and, more important, the more one wants to do, forever seeking the turtle beneath the turtle.

Of what does this cultural analysis consist? This question brings to my mind a Raymond Devos sketch in which he complains of the absence of an announcer and of the difficulty of introducing oneself, because "if I tell them my name, they'll say they already know it, and if I don't tell them, they'll say, 'who's he?'" I have the same feeling concerning cultural analysis. I will, nonetheless, risk an explanation.

There may be as many definitions of cultural analysis as there are anthropologists. I am therefore not going to get entangled in the history of cultural analysis or in a comparative study of the French and American conceptions of it. I will simply explain as clearly as possible what I mean by it. Very plainly, I see cultural analysis as a means of perceiving as "normal" things which initially seem "bizarre" or "strange" among people of a culture different from one's own. To manage this, I must imagine a universe in which the "shocking" act can take place and seem normal, can take on meaning without even being noticed. In other words, I must try to enter, for an instant, the cultural imagination of the other.

The road leading to this point, however, is long and tricky. From the start, we are caught in what seems to be an insolvable problem. On the one hand, since we know more about the world (thanks to anthropology, travel, cinema, television, tourism, immigration, wars of independence, and ethnic and civil rights movements), we are aware of differences, and we fight for the right to maintain these differences. On the other hand, the (justified) fear of racism and its hideous consequences incites us to maintain forcefully that we are all the same, universal human beings. We constantly fall into the trap of wanting to reconcile these two truths; we are caught between the desire to deny differences (we are all human) and the desire to emphasize them (the right to be different). Yet this problem exists only from an ethical perspective. It is indeed when we try to make both of these truths fit into the hierarchy of our value system that we find ourselves in a difficult position.

The problem disappears, however, from the perspective of cultural analysis, which does not concern itself with value judgements. Of course, we are all human. But we speak thousands of different languages, which makes us no less human, and do not find it inconceivable to learn a variety of "foreign" languages. Yet we refuse to accept the idea that we communicate with others through something similar to language, "languages" of which we are unaware—our cultures—despite the fact that we speak a great deal today about cultural differences. Indeed, if I am a cultural being, where is my individuality? Where is my free will? Am I a conditioned and completely predictable being, like a laboratory rat? In order to rid ourselves of these anxieties, we must accept, once and for all, the truth of the following statement: the fact that we are cultural beings in no way implies that we are mere numbers in a series, in no way denies our differences within a common cultural frame of reference. Just as we may speak the same language but never in the same way, so can we participate in a particular cultural milieu and maintain our individuality and our personality.

Indeed, my culture is the logic by which I give order to the world. And I have been learning this logic little by little, since the moment I was born, from the gestures, the words, and the care of those who surrounded me; from their gaze, from the tone of their voices; from the noises, the colors, the smells, the body contact; from the way I was raised, rewarded, punished, held, touched, washed, fed; from the stories I was told, from the books I read, from the songs I sang; in the street, at school, at play; from the relationships I witnessed between others, from the judgments I heard, from the aesthetics embodied everywhere, in all things right down to my sleep and the dreams I learned to dream and recount. I learned to breathe this logic and to forget that I had learned it. I find it natural. Whether I produce meaning or apprehend it, it underlies all my interactions. This does not mean that I must agree with all those who share my culture: I do not necessarily agree with all those who speak the same language as I do. But as different as their discourse may be from mine, it is for me familiar territory, it is recognizable. The same is true, in a certain sense, of my culture.

Part of this logic is tacit, invisible, and this is the most important part. It consists in the premises from which we constantly draw our conclusions. We are not conscious of these premises because they are, for us, verities. They are everything which "goes without saying" for us and which is therefore transparent.

Cultural analysis is necessary only because my culture is not the only one in the world. As soon as there is contact with another culture (and this has always been the case), there is potential for conflict. Indeed, when I meet someone from a culture different from my own, I behave in the way that is natural to me, while the other behaves in the way that is natural to him or her. The only problem is that our "natural" ways do not coincide. Most of the time, though, we get along well, because the fact that our "verities" do not coincide does not mean that they necessarily conflict. The problem only arises, in fact, when there is a conflict. But since it is in the very nature of a verity to be self-evident and not to be challenged, I will not attribute the uneasiness or hurt I feel in a conflict situation to an erroneous interpretation on my part. Instead, I will attribute this difficulty to one, or some, of the other's inherent characteristics. That is to say, following an intercultural experience which bothered or annoyed me without my truly knowing why, or even without my being aware of my discomfort, I will have a tendency to say things like, "The French are . . ." or "Americans are . . .". In other words, if stereotypes are hardy, it is not because they contain a grain of truth but rather because they express and reflect the culture of those who espouse them. Thus when I—a French person—say, "American children are spoiled and impolite," I am not expressing a basic truth but referring rather to the French conception of child raising, which I unconsciously learned to regard as truth, whereas it is merely my (French) truth. When I—an American—say, "French people are rude, they don't let you get a word in edgewise, they interrupt you all the time," I am merely referring to the implicit rules of American conversation. But in order to understand this, I must first become aware of my reading, of the interpretation I bring to the cultural text, of the filter through which I learned to perceive the world. In other words, before learning to understand the culture of the other, I must become aware of my own culture, of my cultural presuppositions, of the implicit premises that inform my interpretation, of my verities. Only after taking this step, which is in fact the most difficult one, can I begin to understand the cultural presuppositions of the other, the implicit premises which inform a formerly opaque text.

The idea that my gaze transforms what I see is very familiar today, almost a cliché. Unfortunately there is a great distance between knowing that my gaze transforms and becoming aware of the ways in which my gaze transforms. Moreover, even if I am ready to recognize the filter which my gaze (taken in its broadest sense) inserts between the world and myself, I will probably attribute it to my artistic sense, or my originality, or my "style," or my way of looking at the world (traits with which I am pleased), or even to my mood (conceiving of it therefore as temporary), thereby affirming and confirming my individuality.

The difficult thing for me to accept is that my gaze is also deeply French (or American) and is therefore similar to other French gazes and recognizable as such. Of course, I know that French table manners are different from those of the Americans or the Chinese. I know that in certain societies it is polite to burp after a meal, I know that in other societies breasts go uncovered but not thighs. I've read, I've seen, I've traveled, I've heard—in short I am a daughter (or son) of this century. But even with that, I have a long road to travel before I can accept that I am a cultural being in my way of loving (not only of making love) and of hating, in my friendships, my dreams, my fantasies, my anger, in all that makes me a human being like all other human beings.

Along this road, two major obstacles. The first, mentioned earlier, is the fear of thinking that I am controlled by an exterior force (which I take to be the culture), that I am transformed into an automation. This fear is dispelled as soon as I realize (a) that my culture is not something external to me, I create it just as it creates me; it is no more outside me than my thoughts; it produces me and I produce it; (b) and that cultural propositions, the premises of which are invisible to me, exist at such a level of abstraction as to allow for and include a very wide range of variations at the level of experience. In other words, two people can act in very different ways and at the same time reaffirm the same cultural proposition at the level of production of meaning. This will be illustrated in the essays that follow.

The second obstacle is completely different from the first. Indeed, it is no longer a matter of resistance but of technique: assuming that I want to become aware of the cultural being that I am, that I want to become aware of my "invisible verities" in order to understand those of the other and to avoid intercultural misunderstandings, how can I go about it? How can I actually do a cultural analysis?

Several anthropologists, Gregory Bateson, Vern Carroll, and Clifford Geertz in particular, have provided models for cultural analysis to which I subscribe, although these models differ on many points. Those who would like to acquire further knowledge of such a theoretical anthropological orientation should read their works. For those who simply (!) want to avoid intercultural misunderstandings, I provide a recipe which is effective yet easy to follow.

The first step consists of clearing the deck, so to speak. I must, above all, avoid all attempts at discovering the deep-seated reasons for the cultural specificity of such-and-such a group. That is to say that I must avoid the temptation of psychological or psychoanalytic explanations ("because American mothers . . . ," "because French people can't stand authority . . . ;") I must also avoid the temptation of explanations that are ecological ("because the Xs lack protein"), geographical ("because they live in the thin mountain air"); meterological ("because of the abundance of rain"), or demographic ("because of the opposition between city and country"). I must avoid the temptation of economic explanations ("because they are capitalists"), of religious explanations ("the French Catholics," "the American Puritans"), of historical explanations (the role of invasions, wars), or even of sociological explanations ("the American family is such because people move around a lot"), and so on. This is not to suggest that these explanations, or different types of analyses, are inferior to cultural analysis. It simply means that they do not deal with culture, that they belong to another domain, as closely connected as that domain may be to culture. Indeed, I am not using cultural analysis to find out why things are as they are or to uncover their deep-rooted nature ("what they are"). Rather, I seek to understand the system of communication by which meaning is produced and received within a group. I seek to discover what things—whether a mode of conduct, an expectation, or a pattern of discourse—mean. I'll come back to this.

The second step consists of being on the lookout. I must, in fact, listen to my own discourse and learn to recognize the value judgments I include when I (sincerely) believe I am simply describing something. The easiest ones to recognize take the form mentioned above: "The French (the Americans/the Japanese) are . . ." followed by an adjective ("arrogant," "vulgar," "cold"). When I do this (and we do it at an incredible pace), I am not describing something but assigning characteristics of my choosing to the other. It is, in fact, the same thing as saying "I find the Xs to be like this or like that," but the assertion "The Xs are . . ." takes the convincing form of a general truth.

Once I can easily identify sentences like these, I must watch out for phrases like "The French (the Indians/the Americans) have no sense of, . . ." "don't know how to, . . ." or other negative expressions which suggest a lack. Indeed, in this case, the only shortcoming for which I am reproaching these Xs is the absence of my culture. What I am saying, in fact, is that the Xs do not have "my" sense of whatever it is.

As soon as we are consciously ready to do so, it becomes easier and easier to notice these statements. The process actually winds up becoming automatic.

Once I become accustomed to operating at this level of awareness,

I can turn to the analysis of a cultural text. What cultural text? It can take almost any form. Linguistic difficulties aside, I am faced with a cultural text when I get a "strange" feeling upon being confronted with an opacity that I cannot dissipate without falling back on the explanation "The Xs are, . . ." which, as we have seen, is anything but an explanation. This can happen to me upon seeing a foreign film, or it can pop up in my daily life, be part of a lived experience. How, then, can I discover the logic that will render this opacity transparent?

First of all, by remembering the experience in detail, by seeing "in slow motion." This requires some effort, because we are generally used to remembering the broad features of an experience, and for the most part we remember them as we have already interpreted them. In the beginning, it might be useful to jot everything down, thereby enhancing memory and allowing for greater detachment. It is even more effective to set aside for a while the "text" thus constructed and to pick it up again later, allowing more and more details to be remembered.

Now that I have the text before my eyes (whether literally or not), it is clearer to me why I found the experience bizarre or unpleasant (it may even have been painful). Putting all that aside, I must try to imagine a context in which this experience is no longer shocking or unpleasant, try to imagine a universe in which what was "bizarre" becomes "normal." Of course, it is not a matter of finding just any interpretation that comes to my mind and which is different from the original one. I must find an interpretation the validity of which can be verified, that is to say, a cultural proposition that is asserted elsewhere in the same culture, though perhaps in a very different form.

Here is an example. One day in Nukuoro, I gave my neighbor a gift: a beautiful piece of cloth. This neighbor was an old woman who was important in the community because of her knowledge of traditions, tales, and legends, and of the native medicine. There was nothing surprising about my action; all kinds of gifts are exchanged almost every day. I will never forget, however, the way in which my gift was received on this occasion. The woman threw my beautiful piece of fabric aside, then began literally to "bawl me out" for having given it to her. I went back to my house, very shaken and close to tears. A present which I had taken such care in choosing, thousands of miles from this island where all I thought one could buy was copra . . . My first reaction was to wonder why she was upset with me, what I had done to anger her, in what serious way I had transgressed common practice (with which I thought I was well acquainted). Then I decided that my reaction was probably ethnocentric, that I had to look elsewhere. At that point, I could have imagined all kinds of explanations different from my first interpretation—for example, that she had not eaten yet that day and that she was in a bad mood. Yet it is obvious that this type of explanation would be purely fanciful, difficult to justify, and, moreover, not useful.

I saw this old woman's daughter, one of my principal informants, shortly after this incident, and she put me on the right track. She had already seen my gift at her mother's house (it is a very small village, and the incident occurred thirty or forty yards from my house). Upon mentioning the gift, which according to her was very beautiful, she asked me if her mother had bawled me out (the Nukuoro expression would be the equivalent of "boiled over") and, without waiting for a reply, told me not to worry if she had, that her mother liked the fabric very much, and that she would most certainly wear it to church the following Sunday (proof that she had appreciated the gift and that she wanted other people to see it).

Why, then, had she screamed at me? It obviously wasn't because of me, or because of my taste. I therefore had to examine the meaning given exchange and gifts in Nukuoro. Who gives gifts to whom? In what circumstances? What type of gifts? As I asked myself these questions, it became more and more clear that by offering a gift, I had put myself in a position of "superiority," if only temporarily, to the extent that I was the one who was giving and she receiving. (The analysis should be much more detailed and refined, but this should suffice here as an example.) Basically, we can say that by screaming and becoming indignant, she was reestablishing the former order: she had no need of this cloth, which she treated as if it were insignificant, and she accepted it, in a sense, to make me happy, because by refusing it she would have insulted me and cut off the nearly familial ties we had established and which she obviously wanted to maintain since she had accepted the gift. When I thought back over the old woman's discourse, I also remembered that she had said something like, "Why are you giving me this? Is it because I told you the legend of Vave? Is it because I brought you some taro?" and so on. By reciting a long list, she reminded me that I hadn't exhausted my debt to her, that I was therefore still her "inferior" (as a child would be), that I was still tied to her. And this conduct was obviously "normal" for a person from Nukuoro, as I later verified, although no one else had acted in such an extreme fashion.

The preceding is an example, an extremely abridged example, of the way cultural analysis functions. By finding my interpretation in the meaning of the gift, I gave myself the possibility of verifying the validity of this interpretation in other areas of this culture.

The next step in cultural analysis consists of trying to discover, by analyzing other experiences, written texts (newspapers, novels, advertisements, civil codes), or oral texts (tales and legends, films, conversations), other domains in which the same cultural proposition seems to be confirmed, but in an apparently different fashion. Thus, the preceding interpretation of the meaning of gift giving was confirmed in a variety of contexts, including, for example, the manner in which a biblical legend had been (unknowingly) transformed by the local church.

Once I become familiar with the technique of analysis, I have only to practice this continual back and forth—"your culture," "my culture"—until it comes easily.

One warning. We are often intimidated by the idea of attempting such a foray into the cultural imaginary of the other, of confidently propelling ourselves into cultural analysis, because we are convinced, deep down, that this constitutes an act of arrogance on our part. Indeed, how can I claim to understand Japanese or German culture if I cannot really understand my neighbor, my parents, my children? Nevertheless, cultural analysis is not an act of arrogance but, quite the contrary, an act of humility by which I temporarily try to forget my way of seeing the world (the only way I have learned to consider valid) and briefly replace it with another way of conceiving this world, a way which by definition I cannot adopt (even if I want to) but the validity of which I assert by this act.

It is easier to understand the nature and goal of cultural analysis, as I understand it, if one thinks of translation. In order to understand a foreign language, I need, metaphorically speaking, a grammar book and a dictionary. Yet these tools are not enough to allow me to penetrate the mysteries of the foreign language: I need to know the meaning of words arranged in a certain way in a certain context. The better I know how to use these two tools, this "grammar book" and this "dictionary," the less I will misinterpret the meaning of the text. And the better I know a language, the more I will be aware not only of the nuances but also of the difficulties, the opacities which previously had not been apparent. All this is nothing new. We all agree on this point, which is why I mention it here. What we accept from translation, which is a difficult but fortunately far from impossible exercise, we have no reason not to accept from cultural analysis. As for translation, the principle is simple (to understand what the foreigner means to say, in his or her own way), though the practice may be ambitious and difficult. As with translation, if I want to make fewer and fewer mistakes in my interpretation of foreigners, I must constantly practice cultural analysis and accept the idea that the more I do, the more I will have to do (and will want to do), and, especially, I must resign myself (and this is the most troubling part) to the fact that I will never attain "the" truth, but "a" truth.

What may require the most practice is the ability to determine where the opacity lies. Because not everything is opaque; on the contrary, the vast majority of intercultural exchanges occur without a hitch. Just as it is possible to "get by" in a foreign language, even to speak it "fluently" but remain totally incapable of producing a good translation of a text in this language, it is also possible to learn all sorts of explicit rules and to respect them (even while doing violence to one's own feelings). One can live for a long time in a foreign country, speak the language, and make many "friends," without ever really understanding their culture, without ever really ridding oneself of a certain division between "them" (that is, those who are "bizarre" in some way) and "us" (adaptable, but guardians of a better system). This tendency is visible among immigrants who arrive in a country as a couple or a family and develop a *modus vivendi* between the home culture and the exterior culture. This juxtaposition is not only possible but frequent when only some members of the family (breadwinners or young children) shuttle back and forth between the two cultural worlds. But as soon as I remove these (protective?) barriers from my daily life, whether I encounter this other culture in my work, in my friendships, in my romantic relationships, in my neighborhood, my market, my temple, or in the education of my children, I have thousands of occasions to experience intercultural misunderstanding, to interpret in my own way an act or a discourse that pertains to a different way of doing things and that requires a different filter; thousands of occasions to treat an opacity as it if it were transparent. Hence, the small (and sometimes deep) wounds, which are all the more painful as we do not know to attribute them to an intercultural misunderstanding; we therefore attribute them to the other's faults or to our own inadequacies. It is indeed within the realm of interpersonal relationships where one feels the most secure, the least guarded— among friends, among lovers, among colleagues, among those closest to us—that cultural misunderstanding has the greatest chance of arising. This is so because we erroneously think that in this domain we are all basically the same—Americans, French, all universal beings. We are, in fact, not the same, but this is far from catastrophic. Indeed, one of the greatest advantages of cultural analysis, aside from that of expanding our horizons, is that of transforming our cultural misunderstandings from a source of occasionally deep wounds into a fascinating and inexhaustible exploration of the other.

As soon as I become aware of all the preceding, what is left (the practice) demands patience and a great deal of intellectual discipline, but it is not difficult from a methodological point of view. It is, nonetheless, a strenuous, sometimes exhausting undertaking from an emotional point of view. Cultural analysis can be more painful than psychoanalysis, as painful as the latter may be. It occurs through a questioning of the very tissue of my being, and it demands an effort which is all the more difficult as I am perfectly integrated into my group and function within it without difficulty. It is also an undertaking which I must accept with the knowledge that I can never completely change my way of being and thinking, which has become entirely involuntary and necessary to me, like breathing. This means that, like it or not, I may find certain traits in myself which I have noticed in other members of my culture; that I may also discover a relationship, which I will find despicable, between certain members of my culture whom I disapprove of or even hate, and myself. This also means that I am, in a sense, going to alienate myself from myself, examine myself when I least expect it.

But these anxieties should not be blown out of proportion. Whatever I do, I will continue to react as I have always reacted. The only difference is that I will be better able to understand my "spontaneity" without in doing so losing it. And when it comes to understanding quickly a misunderstanding that hurt me, made me angry, or disappointed me, cultural analysis is a great advantage. When it comes to discovering the imaginary worlds of others, to discovering other worlds, it offers an enrichment I wish for everyone.

In the following pages I will present my analysis, my interpretation of certain misunderstandings which occur regularly between Americans and the French. I concentrated on analyzing a few aspects of our interpersonal relationships and on discovering the different cultural premises that inform these personal relationships. There, indeed, lies the source of intercultural misunderstanding. I chose the French and American cultures because they are the ones with which I live and which I have spent years studying. But the principles on which these essays are based are applicable to the meeting of any cultures. I hope that others will find this work useful in their own lives and will continue it and expand upon it. It is only a beginning; we are only at the first turtle.

A word of caution: I chose to say "I" to represent others as well as myself. It will therefore be possible to find sentences juxtaposed in my text in which "I" is sometimes masculine, sometimes feminine, sometimes French, sometimes American, sometimes singular, sometimes plural.

# 1   Home

Several years ago, an American anthropologist returning from France, where he had spent the summer on his way back from Africa, told me that what had really struck him was the distrustfulness of the French, who always kept their shutters closed. Just the idea of shutters . . . They made the streets particularly gloomy, as if the villages were uninhabited, or as if people were spying on you from behind them (This anthropologist did not do research in France.)

When my mother came to visit me in the United States, she liked the style of American houses, the way they stood separate from each other, the big lawns, the architectural diversity, the space. One day, we were quietly seated in the living room when she suddenly became aware of the large bay window and, visibly shocked, said to me, "My goodness, you live in the street!" And I understood exactly what she was feeling. It took me years to get used to "living in the street." And when I stroll around my neighborhood in the evening, I am still somewhat surprised at being able to see right into each home. People read, watch television, throw parties, eat dinner, do the dishes, or whatever without closing their drapes, and they are apparently not the least bit bothered by the possibility of a stranger's eyes peering into their lives. And even today, I'm the one who always closes the drapes in our home, much to the amusement of my American husband.

The lawns surrounding American houses display this same refusal to separate the street and the house. In certain American cities the sidewalk itself disappears, the lawn ends where the street begins, and the owner of the house is responsible for its upkeep (as he or she would be for the upkeep of the sidewalk). Space substitutes for walls, railings, or fences, which are sometimes replaced by bushes or trees. But the cutoff point is not clearly defined. Thus, in spring and summer, it is common to see passing strollers sit awhile on your lawn to rest, without, however, going beyond an implicit limit. Backyards and gardens blend into each other in certain small American cities, but more often they are separated by low hedges, across which neighbors exchange produce from their gardens or simply chat. According to an old American tradition, when a family moves into a neighborhood the neighbors immediately come to welcome them, bringing hot coffee and cakes. I benefited from this type of welcome in two different cities, each with over one hundred thousand inhabitants. (I'm speaking here about moving into houses, not apartments.)

We can therefore understand an American's surprise when faced with the walls, gates, shutters, and drawn curtains that "protect" French houses, as well as the uneasiness of a French person before these "open" American houses. But these differences do not really cause any problems. It is inside the house that blunders or misunderstandings have a greater chance of arising.

Dick and Jill are invited to dinner at Pierre and Jeanne's. The conversation becomes lively during cocktails. Pierre speaks enthusiastically about a book he thinks would interest Dick a great deal. He has it fact, and goes to look for it in his study. He is taken aback, as he heads toward the room, when he realizes that Dick is following him. Jeanne goes to the kitchen to check if something is burning. She is just as taken aback when she sees Jill walk in right behind her. Jill offers to help. "No, no thank you, everything is ready . . ." Or at the end of the meal, Jill gets up to clear the table and carries the dishes into the kitchen, or else Dick offers to do the dishes. Pierre and Jeanne protest; if they are unfamiliar with American habits, they might very well consider Jill and Dick to be "intrusive" or "inconsiderate," or they might be "ashamed" that Dick or Jill has seen the rooms "in a terrible mess." ("But what could I do? I wasn't expecting him to follow me all over the house, I didn't know how to stop him.") In fact, it would have sufficed to say "I'll be back in a minute" for Dick not to have gotten up, for him not to have felt obliged to accompany Pierre because Pierre was going out of his way for him.

French people are often surprised when, the first time they enter an American home, their hosts show them around the house, and they interpret this as "showing off." Without excluding this possibility, it is important to understand that an American considers this an attempt to make you "feel at home" by immediately giving you an opportunity to orient yourself, so to speak. Thus, instead of taking your coat when you arrive at a party, the host will show you in which bedroom and on what floor "the coats go." This, among other things, allows you to check your hair, or whatever you like, in the bathroom mirror next door. And if the party is a success, it will spill over into every room on the ground floor, with a definite preference for the kitchen. Guests serve themselves at the bar set up for the occasion (unless the party is more "formal"), help themselves to beer from the refrigerator—in short, they try hard to do as much as they can by themselves so as not to "bother" their host, who also has a right to have fun. This means that the cupboards and drawers are likely to be opened and closed freely, which would give French people the sense that they were being "intruded upon" or that their guests had "been all over the place."

These few examples, and there are many others, already show how different the relationship to the home is in these two cultures.

A French informant told me that he had never entered the kitchen at his grandmother's house, where he ate lunch once a week, until she became very old and less mobile and resigned herself to sending him to get things from the kitchen during meals. While the division between public and private is clearly marked outside the house by its division from the street, thanks to the walls, gates, and drawn curtains mentioned earlier, it is not so clearly marked inside the French home. But the dividing line, though implicit, exists just the same.

One can, in fact, determine the degree of intimacy between two people if one knows to which rooms one person has access in the other's house. The unknown person, the stranger, stays at the door. The next step consists in access to the foyer, then to the living room, then to the dining room (and, if need be, to the toilet). Many visitors will never go any further. A child's friends may have access to the room of that child, as well as to the kitchen for something to drink or for a snack, if they are regular guests in the house. The bathroom, which is separate from the toilet, is off-limits and is reserved for those who could be invited to spend the night. The refrigerator, the closets and the drawers are rarely accessible, except to those considered to be true "intimates" of the house. The room that remains sacred is the parents' bedroom. Of course we are talking about a house that has all these rooms, but space is not the significant factor in this context.

Rather, it is the way in which this space is opened, or not opened, to all those who are not part of the "immediate" family (comprised of the parents and children). Thus, if my father-in-law or mother-in-law, or even my father or mother, lives under my roof, that does not automatically give him or her access to my bedroom. On the contrary. "Well brought up" French people know all this. But one can easily imagine the misunderstandings that can arise when Americans are invited to French homes or when they live (as students) with French families for a period of time.

Similarly, there are misunderstandings in the reverse direction, which may seem surprising given the "relaxed" attitude with which Americans receive guests. A French writer, whose name I will not mention, wrote a book explaining Americans to the French. He enthusiastically tells us that when the lady of the house receives you wearing curlers, it is precisely to make you relax and "feel at home." No problem up to that point. The writer, grateful and admiring, describes the comfort of the room reserved for him, mentions the small touches like letter paper and stamps on the desk. Then the maid (rather a rare character, except in certain social spheres) asks him if he is going to dine with his hosts, and what he would like for dinner. The first evening, he tells us, he goes down to eat with his hosts. Then the second evening, because of the "relaxed" attitude and "kindness" of his hosts, and because he has a great deal of work to do, he decides to eat dinner in his room and "orders a steak and french fries from the maid."

If the writer in question actually did this, his hosts undoubtedly respected his wishes. But it is also more than likely that they attributed his request to "the well-known arrogance" of the French, or at least that they were deeply shocked by the "vulgarity" of this French person, whom, nevertheless, they would never think of enlightening as to his "monstrous" blunder. (The two questions he was asked probably mean "Are you planning to go out for dinner?" and "We'll do our best to please you," or something of that nature.) An unfortunate misunderstanding crowns the best of intentions in this case: the writer-character comes off as a boor, whereas it is his enthusiasm for American hospitality (as he understands it) that makes him unknowingly behave in an impolite fashion.

The misunderstanding is easy to comprehend. Indeed, when you are a house guest in an American home, your hosts immediately show

you your room, the "bathroom" (which includes the toilet), the place
where towels are kept (or where you can get new ones, if there are
already some in your room), the kitchen, including everything you
need to make a cup of coffee or tea if you wake up in the middle of the
night, and, finally, the refrigerator. At the same time, they invite you
to "make yourself at home" and to "help yourself to anything you
want." It is therefore possible that one's enthusiasm for "so much
openness" might leave one with the impression of having all the
advantages of a hotel at home, and that this would result in one's
taking the invitation not to stand on ceremony literally. It is, in fact,
almost impossible, without cultural analysis, to know where the line is
drawn, a line which remains completely implicit. All the Americans
to whom I told this story were shocked by the blunder, surprised that
such a mistake was possible. One need only, however, carry the logic
beyond the invisible line to make such an error.

An American student who spent a year living with a French family
told me that an uncomfortable situation had developed toward the end
of her stay, that there had been a kind of estrangement, for reasons
which she did not understand. After she answered all kinds of questions from me, we reconstructed the misunderstanding as follows. At
the beginning of her stay, as she did not yet know the family, she spent
a good deal of time chatting with the mother and children on returning from school, before going to work in her room. Since she didn't
feel quite comfortable yet, she kept the door to her room open. Much
later, when she thought that she had become "a member of the
family" and really felt at home, she (unconsciously) began acting
exactly as she did at home. That is, on returning from school, she
simply said hello and went directly to her room to work, automatically
closing one door. It was at this point that the family, who must have
felt she was rejecting them without understanding why, began to treat
her with greater distance, "like a foreigner." Only after our discussion
did she realize that what was for her a kind of compliment to the
family (they made her feel at home) was on the contrary an insult
(undeserved, and therefore all the more baffling) to the family, who
had treated her as one of them.

Another student, this time one who lived in a small hotel which
had been transformed into a residence for foreign students, told me of
an unpleasant experience which she didn't understand. This story,
once again, involves a door. One Saturday morning, as neither she

nor her roommate had classes, they told the cleaning woman that they would make their beds themselves because they wanted to sleep late. The cleaning woman, according to them, left looking very angry. The following Saturday, in order to assure that they would not be awakened, they put a "do not disturb" sign on the outer doorknob. This in no way stopped the cleaning woman, who knocked and entered. The two young women didn't stop her, because "the only other solution, which is very difficult for Americans, would have been to tell her to leave." What shocked them most of all was that the cleaning woman knocked and entered almost simultaneously, without giving them a chance to answer. What they considered to be an inviolable space, a room with a closed door, was simply invaded, as if by right. The student who told me of this experience summarized the source of the misunderstanding in this way: "In France, people knock on the door to announce that they are entering, whereas in the United States, it is to ask for permission to enter (for which one must wait) or to make certain the room is empty." I myself remember that, after having spent several years in the United States, I was shocked when a new colleague, who had just arrived from France, knocked and "barged into" my office. Everyone else waited for a "come in," including French people who had been living in the United States for a longer period of time.

A young American, who was boarding with a family in the sixteenth arrondissement in Paris, began, he says, to "behave like a member of the family" until the day when, to his great disappointment, the mother told him that she had rented him the room for purely economic reasons and not to establish a quasi-familial relationship with him. He could not understand how one could have someone in one's home and at one's table and at the same time treat that person "like a stranger." In an equivalent case in the United States, a family who rents a room to a student gives him access to the kitchen ("kitchen privileges") but not to the dining table without a special invitation. A permanent invitation to share the family meal calls for "member of the family" behavior, which undoubtedly explains why the "pension" system does not exist nowadays in most places.

A French student in the United States explained to another French woman, in my presence, that she had moved into a room she liked very much and which an American professor, known for his fine cooking, rented to her. When the woman asked if she ate with the professor's family, the student protested, with both an amused and indignant air, "Oh, no! He made it clear that meals were not part of the deal, and that I shouldn't feel tempted, no matter what kinds of smells emanted from the kitchen. . . . He promised to invite me to dinner. . . . I can't wait." The dividing line had been clearly indicated in this particular case—a rare occurrence. But this clarification did not seem to have prevented the French student from feeling somewhat ruffled, so difficult it is to get used to the assumptions of others. It is all the more difficult for a French person to understand this attitude, since "everyone knows" that Americans invite "people they meet on the street" to dinner, "warmly" open their homes to people they hardly know, easily lend their houses to friends so that friends of their friends, whom they don't know, can use it in their absence. The nonexistence of the boarding system can be explained by the fact that an American will easily put his possessions and himself at your disposal if you are his guest but will not agree to "sell" you his services right inside his home, to give you the rights of a "paying customer" over him and over his freedom. In the French family, everyone usually eats dinner together. The meal must therefore be prepared in any case, and one more person at the table doesn't make much difference. In the American family, on the other hand, it is possible for each family member to eat dinner separately on certain evenings, when it is most convenient for her or him, because schedules are often difficult to coordinate. Having a boarder and owing him or her a meal every day would demand more of the "parents" than the children do themselves.

It is now clear that French and American houses differ not only on the exterior. Their differences are in fact reproduced, but less visibly, inside the house. The distinct separation between the inside and the outside in French culture anticipates the barriers to be crossed once inside. Access to different rooms denotes the path toward intimacy, so to speak, and corresponds to the visible/invisible division. What I mean is that the rooms which are "off limits" are closed and hidden from the eyes of those who have not been specifically admitted. By the same token, someone who stands close to a window, perfectly visible from the street, should adopt an "outside" form of behavior, even though he is separated from the outside by the window.

On the other hand, the American house is as open to strangers as it is visible from the street. In the evening, lit up on a dark street, it even attracts attention. If this does not seem to bother an American, it is because such openness in no way encroaches on his privacy, which he defines by setting up the barriers of his choice—by closing the door to his room, by surrounding himself by huge lawns or thick trees, by refusing all boarders, or simply by stopping you on your way to a room by saying "I'd rather you didn't see the mess," or "I'll be right back." Fences, walls, and high hedges give him the impression of being closed in and seem to deprive him of the spectacle of the street, the forest, or the beach bordering his house. And he will consider as an invasion of his privacy any instrusion made without his knowledge or against his wishes (electronic surveillance, of course, but also a door opened without waiting for permission, and the like). An American colleague does not enter your office without being invited: he or she remains on the threshold, even if the door is wide open. If your window is near the street, passersby will make it their business "not to see you," and if by chance your gazes meet through the window, they will smile or make a friendly gesture as if to say that they were looking into your house "by accident."

If I take the logic of the preceding analysis to its limit, I obtain two literally inverse situations. In French culture, the person who enters my house is responsible for knowing the rules, for remaining within the spatial limits that our relationship authorizes. (Thus I must be wary of a stranger who would invite me to skip some steps, to penetrate the depths of his house immediately.) I therefore have no defense against guests who feel "at ease" in my home, like Americans who follow me into the kitchen. In American culture, on the other hand, I am the one who is responsible for indicating the limits beyond which a person entering my house must not venture. What is troubling for French people is that these limits can change according to my mood. Here is an example: Tom (American) is putting up the parents of his wife (French), who are vacationing in the United States. On certain evenings, Tom is "charming" and sociable, whereas on others he comes from from work, barely says hello, takes a beer from the refrigerator ("without even offering them one"), sinks into his chair, and reads the paper. In this case, Tom, for personal reasons which, according to American culture, he need not explain, is indicating that he does not want his "space," his privacy, to be invaded. It is very probable that Tom would behave in exactly the same way in the absence of his in-laws, that his desire for solitude has nothing to do with them. But the in-laws, not knowing how to interpret this message, are hurt and do not understand why Tom "has them at his home, only to treat them this way."

As we can see, hardly have we crossed the threshold when the intercultural misunderstandings begin. We can easily imagine that these won't be the last.

# 2 Conversation

We are driving in a car. X (French) is taking me home. It is not for the first time, and, what is more, X is quite familiar with the city. Yet X seems to be unsure of the correct route to follow and asks me questions which obviously do not call for an answer, since he asks them just as he is taking the action which the answer could influence—for example, "Do I turn here?" just as he is turning. Often, commentaries on the car, the road, other cars, and surprising expressions of concern come from behind the wheel ("Do you think I have enough gas?"; "What's this guy doing, is he going to change lanes or not?"; "I'm sure we can't squeeze between these two cars, but I'm gonna try"; "I should have gone the other way, we'd be there already"; etc.). X's case is not unique. I've witnessed many variations on this scene. The participants were men as well as women, young as well as old. As soon as I became aware of it, I even caught myself "in the act."

Do French people speak without saying anything, as Americans sometimes accuse them of doing? Is X's pseudomonologue as devoid of meaning as it seems?

Another context: a party, in a university town in the United States, in honor of a well-known French academic. The host and most of the guests are French. There are a few scattered Americans. The French academic, who has just been introduced to an American historian, looks interested. "I'm very interested in history . . . Are you familiar with Z (famous American historian)?" "Yes." "What do you think of his latest book?" The American responds, talking about what he thinks of the book in question. The Frenchman, having stopped listening at a certain point, is glancing around the living room, and he eagerly widens the circle when another Frenchman approaches and "brutally interrupts" the conversation with a joke. The newcomer turns to the American, "What are you working on right now?" The latter, who has learned his lesson, responds briefly with "Oh, the same thing" and makes a joke.

This little scene was described to me by the American in question, who added, "I really don't understand French people; they only pretend to ask questions. This behavior especially surprised me coming, as it did, from such a famous man. He had no need to ask the question if he wasn't interested in the answer. Of course I wasn't going to fall into the same trap twice, so I joked 'French-style' instead of answering."

Americans often expressed surprise in my presence at the fact that French people, "who claim to be very big on manners," are themselves so "rude": "they interrupt you all the time in conversation," "they finish your sentences for you," "they ask you questions and never listen to the answer," and so on. French people, on the other hand, often complain that American conversations are "boring," that Americans respond to the slightest question with a "lecture," that they "go all the way back to Adam and Eve," and that they "know nothing about the art of conversation."

The mutual accusations come up often enough to claim our attention. What they indicate must be a cultural phenomenon, opaque to the foreigner. They suggest a profound difference in the interpretation of conversation—a daily activity which appears clear-cut, familiar, and immediately accessible. But although the word "conversation" is the same in French and in English, it is far from signifying the same thing in the two cultures. That there is misunderstanding is moreover apparent in the fact that the (French) journal *Communications* dedicated an entire issue to this subject (no. 30, 1979), without for an instant stopping to consider the fact that the theory of H. Paul Grice, which served as a point of departure for many chapters, applies to the American model but not to the French one. The implicit character of the theory having naturally escaped French researchers, more than one of them attacked it, after having implicitly presented it as universal. (As Grice's text was written in English, it is difficult to know if he was aware of its cultural implications. I do not, however, believe that he saw its cultural limitations.)

What does conversation mean to the French? In French, we say that a conversation must be "engaged," "sustained," "fueled," and "revived" if it is "dragging," "rerouted" if it is "dangerous." Once we permit a conversation to begin, we owe it to ourselves to keep it from dying, to care for it, to guide it, to nourish it, and to watch over its development as if it were a living creature. This is enough to suggest the importance we place on conversation, but it does not explain the meaning we attribute to it, that is to say, why we give it this importance.

Let's see what happens in a simple conversation between two French people. I (the speaker) look at my interlocutor, watch for signs of boredom or inattention. If the other person's gaze begins to stray, to wander, I change my behavior, my tactic, or the subject, or else I cut myself short to allow him or her to speak. Of course, we are not talking about what truly happens in most cases but of the norm, the "ideal" situation which remains unchanged, no matter how often the rule is broken. In the inverse case (someone is speaking to me), I have several means at my disposal to intervene or to indicate that I want to speak: facial expressions, lips which open as if to say something but remain silent, slight body movements, or gestures. If this does not obtain the desired result and I still am unable to speak, I must make use of other signs—a barely audible inhalation which indicates that I am going to speak, a discreet sigh, a chopped-off word—or the stratagems of last resort—"speaking of which" "funny you should mention that"— which in general have nothing to do with the preceding conversation but rather indicate that I would like to say something too. If I start to look distracted or take on a vacant stare, it is to indicate, in what is still an acceptable manner, that I am ready to abandon the conversation since there is no place in it for me. If this has no effect, my only hope lies in the intervention of a third party (a friend met fortuitously on the street, a host or hostess, a guest, or a table companion at a meal or party) to save me from this "pain in the neck." If worse comes to worst, I can avail myself of the excuses that have the disadvantage of being obvious: a telephone call to make, something urgent to tell someone else that I almost forgot, and the like. When I am pushed to this extreme, I am really resentful at the other for having "cornered" me, for having "kept me" (and therefore held me against my wishes), for having "monopolized the conversation" for "hours"—in short, for not having "given" me a chance to speak, that is, for having refused me all meaningful presence.

The fact that I allowed X to "hold me back" in this way suggests that something else was holding me back, something stronger than my impatience or my boredom, something I call manners but which encompasses an entire gamut of implicitly accepted social obligations. What is more, the many signals at my disposal for attracting X's attention, and to which X should be sensitive and respond, suggest that the relationship between two people engaged in conversation is more important than the mere subject of the conversation, more important than the amount of information exchanged. This assertion is confirmed, I believe, in the case of conversations in which one "strays from the topic." I would say that whoever brings up a topic is completely free to stray from it and does so, most often, by the intermediary of "that reminds me of . . . ," "why just the other day . . . ," "that makes me think of . . . ," and so on. These departures from the topic, these "side trips," so to speak, allow the conversants to continue speaking while holding at bay the need for the signs of intervention mentioned earlier. There is, in a sense, a suspension of conversational expectations, just as we follow without complaining someone who gives us a tour of his garden and draws our attention to such and such a path. Meanwhile, it is possible for the other conversants to intervene, and to speak in turn, simply by means of "to get back to . . . ," though they are not obliged to return to the original topic. In fact, someone who shows a certain insistence on returning to a topic would be considered boorish or childish, desirous of drawing attention to himself, and would create an annoyance (or worse, a rupture in the conversation).

Here again, the important thing is to establish ties, to create a network, tenuous as it may be, between the conversants. The exchange of words, in the "thread" of conversation, serves to weave these ties between the speakers. If we imagine a conversation as being a spider's web, we can see the exchanging of words as playing the role of the spider, generating the threads which bind the participants. The ideal (French) conversation would resemble a perfect spider's web: delicate, fragile, elegant, brilliant, of harmonious proportions, a work of art. If there are many more perfect spider's webs than there are ideal conversations, it is because the spider is alone in weaving its web, whereas conversations require at least two participants. The danger and the risk of error are thus far greater (sometimes we even get tangled in the web). The character of a particular conversation and its form therefore reflect, with a great deal of exactitude for whoever takes the trouble to read the signs, the nature of the relationship between the conversants. We create the fabric of our relationship in the same way and at the same time that we "make" conversation.

Thus, for example, if I run errands in the neighborhood, I'll "chat a bit" with the owners of the shops where I usually go. If I pick up my children at school, I'll do the same with parents whose children are in the same class as mine, and with the teacher if I see him or her. With the shopkeepers, I'll probably talk about the weather, our health, about the hard times (if they are so), about my family's preference for a particular product, about the beautiful variety of fruits, about an event which occurred in the street near the store, and so on. The closer our ties, the longer the conversation will be (within the limits imposed by the context, customers who are waiting, the time of day, etc.). With other parents, I will speak briefly about our children, about school, about the weather and about the most recent flu epidemic, unless there is something to organize (a meeting, a party). The conversation will rarely be a long one, as each of us is in a hurry to get back, to bring the children home. The length of the conversation will be limited by the circumstances (and the number of parents grouped together at the same time), and the nature of the conversation will be a direct reflection of the nature of our relationship (a polite, friendly, or warm exchange). In any case, it is important for there to be some sort of exchange, short as it may be. This explains why someone might say, "My God, I saw Madame Z outside the school, but I didn't even have time to stop and say a few words. What must she think?" In such a case, an American would have said "Hi," and that would have sufficed. Thus the American's surprise at "the time we spend" chatting with one another.

Another source of incomprehension for Americans: it is not only possible, but frequent, if I live in an apartment building with an elevator for example, for me to hold the door and say hello to my upstairs or downstairs neighbor (or even a next-door neighbor) and for us to ascend eight or fifteen flights together without saying another word to each other (except goodbye), perhaps even on a daily basis. But for me (French) there is no contradiction between the way I have

conversations in my neighborhood and the fact that I hardly speak to
my immediate neighbors: it is only by chance that we live so close to
each other, and this is not a sufficient reason for us to develop a
relationship, unless of course we specifically choose to do so. Similarly, on a small, quiet, provincial street, it suffices for me to nod my
head and to say hello to the neighbors who live next door and across
the street (unless an extraordinary event interrupts the routine).

In the same way, while a customer's "hello" or "goodbye," in
France, is directed at everyone in the store, conversation occurs only
between the customer and the shopkeeper, and not among customers
(even if they see each other there every day), unless it occurs through
the intermediary of the shopkeeper ("Why don't you ask Madame Z")
or because of an exceptional event (an accident, a demonstration in
the streets). A better example of this situation can be seen in cafés. I
have several choices in a café. I can go with someone, remain at the
counter, and speak only to my companion; I can meet friends there, in
which case we sit at a table, or the first one to arrive sits at the table we
will occupy. We talk among ourselves. I can also go alone and take a
table if I want "to be left alone," and I can read, write a novel, or write
letters, without speaking to anyone except the waiter (and even then,
only to order). If, however, I do nothing but drink whatever it is I am
drinking and look around me (or at someone in particular) insistently,
I give the impression that I am there for a "pickup" (a continual source
of problems for unsuspecting American women). If I feel like having a
conversation, I'll settle in at the counter, where I can chat only with
the owner of the café or whoever is standing behind the counter. I can
also start up a conversation with someone at the counter, but only via
the café owner, and only if I am already a regular customer; if not, my
move will seem suspicious. This is why the café owner must know
how to "talk" with all kinds of people. Every day, in a small café in La
Rochelle (where I conducted many interviews), students, workers,
policemen, and employees rub elbows. The café owner described the
situation in these terms: "You don't need a fancy education to own a
café, to talk with people . . . about everything. . . . Even if you don't
know much about it, you can still talk. . . . The café is a place where
people meet each other. . . . We talk . . . about business, sports,
work, about granny's illness . . . about anything. . . . They have
their little habits which we're familiar with; we make friends more or
less, with some of them. . . . They all get along just fine . . . stu-

dents, cops, they manage to agree." Then, underlining the essential role which the café owner plays in these unexpected exchanges (between students and cops, for example), he continues, "it really depends on the person behind the counter. . . . People come for the ambience of the café, but also for the person who's behind the counter. . . . That's what determines the clientele, in fact."

An experienced observer has no problem recognizing the clientele, the regulars, as we can see if we go back to the example of the shopkeeper, an example which has the advantage of being readily accessible, of being observable by everyone, even by those who rarely go to cafés. In a small Parisian bakery in which I made many recordings, I was able to hear an entire gamut of conversations between the bakery owner and her customers within just a few hours. If we exclude the polite exchanges common to all of them ("hello," "please," "thank you," "goodbye"), we can quickly distinguish a few telltale signs. For example, the purely informational exchanges ("What would you like?" "A *baguette*" "Well-browned?" "Yes." "Here you are, it's such-and-such a price") clearly indicate the nonregulars; strictly speaking, there was no conversation. The rare regulars who chose not to converse (due to shyness, reserve, misanthropy) were distinguishable from the preceding by the fact that they did not need to be told the price of the bread, or else, and especially, by the gestures of the baker, who turned toward a particular kind of bread while saying, for example, "*un batard* (thick loaf of bread)" or "*une ficelle* (long, thin loaf of bread) as usual?" Otherwise, the regulars were entitled to a conversation, as short as it may have been ("Feeling better today?" in which the "better" and "today" suggest other days, and therefore, economically, the relationship). There are regulars who are addressed as Madame or Monsieur, those who are addressed as Monsieur Z or Madame Z, and then those who are addressed by their first names (and with whom the baker uses the informal "you" form, *tu*). There are those who are asked about the "children" or the "little ones," those who are asked about "your daughter/grandson/wife/mother," and those who are asked about "Gaston," "Nicole," or "Arthurine." There are those who go directly to the counter (they are in a rush, have a brief conversation) and those who wait on the side and let other customers pass (they know the baker rather well, and are going to have a longer, more intimate conversation). And then there are those rare customers who are admitted to the back room (who are asked about all the members of their family, whom the baker refers to and names by their first names, etc.). In this case, the bread is mentioned and purchased almost as an afterthought; it is paid for in the same way, or just added to "the bill" (which these days is a sign of a solid relationship). It seems therefore that between the regular customer and the shopkeeper, conversation transforms what would normally be a purely economic transaction into a social exchange and therefore into a tie to be reinforced or maintained.

It is now clear, I believe, that the French do not talk "without saying anything" and that, on the contrary, French conversation is loaded with meaning, especially in that it affirms and reveals the nature of the ties between the conversers. But in what way does this analysis explain the first situation mentioned at the beginning of this chapter—in what way does this analysis give meaning to X's seemingly "disconnected" phrases while he was driving me home? To understand this monologue, which seems abnormal, we must consider it to be a conversation reduced to the bare essentials, to what is necessary and sufficient in the situation at hand. In fact, the commentaries that X seems to pour out "for no reason" play an important role: they acknowledge my presence. In addition, they reveal that close or fairly close ties already exist between X and me, that we are comfortable enough together not to have to converse if we do not particularly feel like it: X may be a member of my family (my mother, my son, my wife, my brother), a boyfriend or girlfriend, a close buddy, an old friend, and so on. If this were not the case, X would not indulge in his little monologue but would "make" conversation, would engage me in a verbal exchange by asking questions that would require answers rather than questions that, on the contrary, do not call for any, since they are asked, if you remember, at the very moment when the action is taking place ("Do I turn right here?" while turning). If, on the other hand, X, with whom I have close ties, drove me home in silence, it could signify boredom, a bad mood, or anger. The silence might quickly become heavy, menacing—in any case a sign of rejection and of difficulty (unless I know X to be taciturn, "quiet"). If the silence were mutual, due to fatigue, for example, we would, at least briefly, comment upon it ("I'm bushed"; "It's so quiet, so nice") and thereby explain it.

At the other extreme, in the absence of any relationship, silence is neutral, if not hostile. This is why in the elevator, in the street, on the bus, and in practically every place where the other is almost totally foreign to my daily life, where the context does not call for ties to be formed or else lends itself to misunderstandings, "people don't talk to each other readily in France." We can be both complete strangers and completely glued to one another in France, as in the métro during rush hour, or in the airport when the boarding of a plane has been announced but has not yet begun. Speaking is what brings us closer to each other.

This is a seemingly inexhaustible source of misunderstanding between the French and Americans, especially since, to complicate matters, these rules are suspended under exceptional circumstances and on vacation (and therefore on the train, on the plane). It is indeed in public places that Americans in France for the first time have the experience, at times amusing, but often unpleasant and even painful, of cultural misunderstanding. They feel rejected, disapproved of, criticized, or scorned without understanding the reason for this "hostility," and they can draw only one of two conclusions: "the French hate Americans," or "the French are cold (hostile/unpleasant/arrogant/despicable)." And the buried wound becomes an entrenched conviction, constantly reinforced. This is essentially due to the fact that Americans and the French do not attribute the same meaning to verbal exchanges yet believe their meanings to be identical. Thus the astonishment when faced with unexpected results, the incomprehension when faced with disjunction in what should "go without saying."

When one American passes another on the street, in the middle of the day and in a neighborhood not known to be dangerous, there is a good chance, if one exchanges glances with the other, that he or she will smile or nod, or even say hello to the stranger, without it going any further. This often surprises French visitors in the United States. As a respectable, gray-haired man said to me, "If I were younger, I would think all these pretty girls were giving me the eye. . . . They seem like such flirts when they smile at you like that. . . . If this were France . . ." This same sudden and fleeting rapport among strangers can be established just as well through conversation in the United States, here again without consequence. It can even last a long time, as at American dinners and parties, at which one meets "very nice" people, with whom one has long conversations, and whom one will never see again (which French people find deeply disturbing).

In this respect it is interesting to compare what happens in France and in the United States in the supermarket when the store is crowded, with a long line in front of the cash register and a long wait. In France, in most cases, one quickly shows signs of impatience, by raising one's eyes to the ceiling with an exasperated expression, by taking on an exhausted look, by stiffening or clamming up, or by exchanging with others glances of complicity. But one does not speak to others—all is expressed through body movements. At most, one might protest, "grumble" out loud while looking at one's neighbor, but without speaking to him directly. One simply makes him an accomplice against the cashier, the store, the system, those who are "going too far." In the United States, the situation is completely different. One turns to one's neighbors; people strike up rather general conversations, help each other pass the time, and joke about the situation—even sympathize with the cashier—and, when they finally get to the register, encourage the person there with a few kind words. I've seen strangers show each other family photos, exchange advice, recipes, or useful addresses, compare pregnancies and births, all just as calmly as if they were talking about the quality of a product or the use of an unusual vegetable in one's shopping cart. Most of all I've seen them joke around a lot. A French woman who heard me speaking French to a friend I had met in the supermarket introduced herself to us, gave us her address and telephone number, and invited us to come see her if we were passing by the city in which she lived. Then, just before leaving us, she apologized for her behavior by saying, "Excuse me for having come up to you like that, but I heard you speaking French. I've become very American, you know. . . ."

More than once, I have noticed that when the supermarket becomes very crowded, when it is difficult to move around or even to know in which line one is waiting, the atmosphere becomes partylike, fun-filled. And on these occasions, even though there are newspapers and magazines near each register to tempt customers and encourage them to be patient, few people choose to read, unless they mix their reading with conversation (commentaries on the headlines, the sensationalism of certain weeklies, etc.). Indeed, isolating oneself in reading and silence in such a restricted space could, I believe, signify a rejection of others.

A French person could see the confirmation of his stereotypes in all this ("Americans are good-natured," "Americans have superficial relationships," etc.) because for a French person, the following "truth"—or cultural presupposition—is self-evident: conversation commits me to another person, it is a commentary on our relationship, one of the ways at my disposal to make the distinction between those with whom I have, affirm, confirm, or want to create ties, and all the others whose social importance in my life I deny by this refusal. These ties, one should note, are not necessarily pleasant; I may even bitterly regret having them, secretly dream of freeing myself of them, but insofar as I refuse or cannot afford the price of this break, these ties are essential to my social existence, they inscribe me in the social. But all this has settled in my mind unbeknownst to me, and I (as a French person) am generally unaware of possessing these implicit assumptions, this screen through which I see and understand the world. For this perspective, it is "normal" for me to find that Americans display a certain "promiscuity" in their conversations in the supermarket, as they do in their relationships (see the chapter on friendship). It is also "normal" for me to refuse all ties that I have not chosen (in the broadest sense), that have been imposed on me by circumstance, by chance, which assigns me certain neighbors, which places me next to others in the subway, in a store, on the street, in the check-out line at the supermarket, and so on.

Similarly, to the extent that I (as an American) do not feel bound by conversation because of the unconscious screen through which I see the world, I can make conversation almost anywhere with anyone. Furthermore, the nature of my relationship with another person can be determined not by our conversation but by the space I allow between us. The closer our relationship, the less space there will be between us, as is indicated metaphorically by the expression "a close-knit family." Thus, if by chance I find myself in a situation in which the space between another person and myself is smaller than the space which would "normally" express the nature of our relationship (or the absence of one), I can always resort to conversation to recreate the involuntarily diminished distance. If I cannot move away from a person who is literally invading my relational space, I redress the balance with conversation, and all goes well if the other person and I are both American, since we will both "spontaneously" be drawn toward the same solution (the other doesn't want me in his or her relational space either if I am a stranger).

We can now imagine the potential for misunderstanding inherent in a very simple scenario: circumstances put a French person and an

American together in a limited space, at a table in the dining car of a train, for example. The French person will recreate distance with silence, the American with conversation. The degree zero of an American conversation would therefore be the smile I address to a stranger I pass in the street, and with whom I exchange glances—if I look elsewhere, I am not obliged to do anything. But the empty stare, the stare that passes through the other without seeing him or her, is not an American specialty. If I want to avoid the other's gaze, I look elsewhere (as in the New York subways, where it is dangerous to smile blissfully). If my gaze meets the other's gaze and I do not greet him or her, do not smile, or do not quickly look away, this exchange of glances becomes the equivalent of a reduction in our relational space and can take on connotations of seduction or suggest a challenge or insult, depending on the context.

I would like to stop a moment on this question of space. For an American, I repeat, it is the space between oneself and the other that reveals the nature of their relationship, not their conversation. This space is therefore clearly marked for whoever knows how to read the signs. Americans obey these rules automatically, of course, without thinking about them and even without being aware of them, since they have become "natural," which in this case means "cultural." I (an American) will not permit physical contact, and therefore the ultimate reduction in the space between us, except with certain people with whom I have a very close and clearly defined relationship. I can therefore hug (literally, "embrace") my parents, grandparents, brothers and sisters, children, and other members of my family, my friends, my spouse, or my lover. If I embrace a person of the opposite sex, the fact that we pat each other on the back toward the end of the embrace indicates, according to my interpretation, that our relationship is neither a sexual nor a romantic one. (The many Americans to whom I disclosed the role I attribute to this patting on the back, against which the French body rebels, were not even aware of doing it. Many of my students told me they had hurried to verify my theory and to test it out by observing others and themselves, and then confirmed my interpretation, grumbling about it in a friendly way: I had made them aware of a totally "spontaneous" gesture, and suddenly they saw themselves doing it. May the American reader beware of this, and not hold it against me!) Since the days of the hippies, we can observe variations in this pat on the back: young people today may prefer a more or less noticeable swaying from side to side of the two "embracing" bodies. This embrace, tight or loose, long or short, according to the relationship expressed, takes place in silence.

This behavior explains why, when I find myself against my will very near to a person I don't know, I will speak to try to reestablish the distance. Otherwise, if we are in a limited space, or we touch, and I don't say anything, my silence will seem suggestive and become a sexual invitation. This is why the rush hour (French) subway is such a traumatizing experience, since my (American) efforts to reestablish the distance with words correspond, for a French person, to a suggestive invitation. And the accusations of promiscuity fly in both directions (touch anybody, talk to anybody). It is interesting to notice here that when the implicit rule has been broken, it is with words that violence is initiated in the French context and with silent space reduction in the American.

When my space is not threatened, (American) conversation will allow me to "become acquainted" with the other and will give him or her information that will allow him or her to become acquainted with me. But this is true only for the present, within the limits defined by the context, and without any obligation for us to maintain the relationship, since conversation is not a commentary on our relationship but rather an exploration. American conversation is closer to a hike with two or more people in unknown territory than to a game on familiar territory—hence the need immediately to situate the participants (the territory) and the importance of cooperation. Each person will contribute to the exploration according to his or her knowledge and capacities. We may return from this hike with our hands empty or full, depending on the moment, the mood, and the quality of each person's contribution. Consequently, if I (an American) am unsure of my information, I do not pretend to know but let whoever might know more speak. But if I have something to "contribute," I can speak as long as seems necessary to respond to a question, to share my information. And I will listen to the other in the same way when it is his or her turn, no matter what the other's style may be. And since when I am finished, I will spontaneously stop speaking, the other person will wait for this silence, different from that of a thoughtful pause, to speak in turn. Any other kind of behavior would look like an insulting interruption to me; I would interpret it as a sign of lack of interest or, even worse, as frivolous and annoying, as contributing nothing more than

"noise," "senseless commotion," or signs of "impatience" to the conversation. In short, the interruption is more a commentary on the
person who interrupts than on the person who is interrupted. We can
now understand why Americans are shocked by the "rudeness" of
French people who "interrupt you all the time."

But if it is true that in the French context silence allows me to
create distance, it then follows, according to my cultural logic, that
the closer people are, the less silence there will be, and the more the
conversation will be "animated," "lively." We can therefore understand why French people "often ask questions without waiting for an
answer," according to Americans. Seen in its cultural context, this
mode of conduct becomes not reprehensible because impolite but, on
the contrary, normal, that is to say, in conformity with the norm. The
question that is asked, but for which no answer is awaited, is in fact a
way of indicating interest. When I (a French person) ask another
person questions in the course of conversation, it is more to manifest
my interest in him or her than to obtain information, to become
informed. The most obvious example, of course, is "how are you?"
(*comment allez-vous?*), but the gamut of such questions is wide. If, in
addition to showing interest, I really want information, to learn as
many details as possible, I can always ask the question again, formu-
late it in several ways, or make it more specific if the response seems
too vague or if it intrigues me and arouses my curiosity. Hence the
impatience of the French when faced with long, detailed responses,
which "go all the way back to Adam and Eve" or "turn into lectures"
and "monopolize" the conversation. In the French context, it is
therefore the person who provides a literal (and hence overly long)
response to a question who can be accused of being rude. This is a
classic case of intercultural misunderstanding, illustrated by the second situation described at the beginning of this essay. By asking the
American historian his opinion of a particular book, the French academic, at the party in his honor, was simply trying to begin a conversation (in French style) and did not really want an American-style
response to his question (which involves sharing the information one
possesses). If the French person really wanted an opinion on the book,
he would have asked the question much later in the conversation,
after having explained, in one way or another, why one historian's
opinion of another interested him, a nonhistorian who had his own
views on the question, and only after having created a relationship and

thus established the "credibility" (according to him) of his interlocutor and hence the "validity" of his opinion. By asking his question immediately after an introduction, he was merely using it to begin a conversation, "tossing it out" like a ball. Obviously, in this case, one does not expect the other person to keep the ball but to toss it back, and so on.

Long, uninterrupted responses, attentively listened to, are reserved, by French people, for so-called serious conversations, which are out of place at a party, or in any similar context, because they isolate the group that is "talking seriously" from the rest of the possible conversers, who might feel excluded or rejected, and rightfully so. Moreover, if two or three people have this type of conversation within a larger group, they will, whether unconsciously or purposely, spatially isolate themselves from the rest of the group, in the corner of a room, for example. This will be accepted for a while by the other members of the group at hand, who will tacitly understand that they shouldn't "bother them," go near them, or interrupt them. In exchange, these two or three people will tacitly know that they cannot prolong this isolation too long without being "rude," without insulting the rest of the group, which "is going to wonder what's going on" or very simply abandon them to their "heated discussion." It is worth noting that one "has" a serious conversation or a discussion, whereas one "makes" conversation (in French as in English). It is in the context of a serious French conversation that the American will be most at ease because it corresponds most closely to his own definition of conversation.

Even more than the questions that do not require true answers, it is the "continual interruptions" in French conversation that baffle Americans. But, as we should expect by now, what an American takes for an interruption is not really an interruption but plays a completely different role in French conversation. Seen from the exterior, French people engaged in conversation do indeed seem to spend their time interrupting one another. The conversation seems pleasant nonetheless, and the participants give no sign of annoyance, frustration, or impatience (to the French observer, that is). On the contrary, interruptions seem to be a driving force in the conversation. It is therefore permitted, at certain moments and not at others, to interrupt the conversation without being rude. To know which moments are appropriate, one need only consider the "interruption" as a punctuation mark. It is in no way a matter of cutting someone off in the middle of a word or sentence but, rather, of seizing the pause, brief as it may be, to react. I do not interrupt to draw attention to myself or to speak in turn but to show my interest in the other's remark, which merits a commentary, a word of appreciation, denial, protest, or laughter—in short, a reaction, without which the remark would "fall flat." The ball is tossed to be caught and tossed back. When there is no "interruption," when each person speaks sedately in turn (as in American conversation, according to the French), the conversation never "takes off"; it remains polite, formal, cold.

The interruption-punctuations, then, are proof of spontaneity, enthusiasm, and warmth, a source of unpredictability, interest and stimulation, a call for participation and pleasure. They are the ties that bind, that bring the conversants closer together. This explains why very animated conversations (at cafés for instance) are a source of pleasure and stimulation (just like a wild game of soccer on the beach). These conversations take place among people who have already established a relationship (that of being "old regulars" may be sufficient in order to "talk politics"), who meet at the café expecting such conversations. The rhythm of the exchange, the tone of the voices, and the frequency of the laughter are indications of the pleasure that the participants draw from the conversation. The faster the rhythm, the higher the voices go, and the more the exchange is punctuated with laughter, until the final explosion. For an unsuspecting American (and in this case, they are in the majority), the rapidity of the exchange may be interpreted as a series of interruptions (and therefore an indication of aggression) and the tone of the voice as an expression of anger. (When my daughter was little, she asked me one day why I always fought with my French friends who came to the house and never with my American friends; that was probably the day that I began my cultural analyses.) As for the laughter-punctuation, it becomes one more "proof," for an American, that "French people laugh for no reason," "aren't serious." An American will also find it extremely difficult to participate in a French conversation even if he or she speaks French perfectly, which is a very frustrating experience.

Similarly, the rhythm of American conversation, the tone of voice to adopt, and the place for laughter can be forever misunderstood or mysterious. For me (a French person who speaks American fluently), the rhythm is slow and always the same, and my efforts to accelerate the rhythm are constantly submerged in the unalterable wave of words that engulfs those efforts. My laughter will always seem out of place, and my attempts to participate will be treated as untimely interruptions. What may be most difficult to swallow is that the American interlocutor seems blind to all my signals (indicating that I want to speak), may be conscious of them without responding to them, or may go so far as to utter calmly the terribly "insulting" phrase, "Let me finish." And to add to it all, the American interlocutor doesn't even look at me.

Indeed, if we remember, looking someone straight in the eyes means (to the American) invading the other's relational space. I (as an American) will therefore only look at my interlocutor from time to time, without allowing my gaze to "linger." For these same reasons, I am not obliged to look at each conversant one by one (as a French person would do in order to include all those present in the conversation), but only to shoot rapid circular glances at the group. Similarly, if my interlocutor looks elsewhere, this does not necessarily indicate a lack of interest. If, in addition, one of my pauses was interpreted by my interlocutor as the final pause of my discourse (thus it is his or her turn to speak), I can indicate the error simply by saying "I haven't finished" (which is not a reprimand for rudeness, as a French person would interpret it).

The ideal American conversation does not seek to evoke fireworks, as can be the case for French conversation but, in my opinion, is closer to a jazz session, even a "jam session." Just like a jazz musician, who can bring his musical instrument, join a group of musicians he does not know, play with them, and leave, disappearing forever into the night, so I, in theory, can join a conversation if I have something to add, learn from the conversation, and then disappear forever into the night. Just as in a jazz session each musician plays his solo as he wishes, without interruption, so I can speak according to my style and my talent, without interruption. Like the jazz musician, I will have learned, through a long apprenticeship, to recognize the moment when the other person's solo has finished and when to begin (and end) my own. The discordant notes are the loud voices, the "excited" tone, and the laughter "about nothing," which hinder the understanding and accord necessary for the group to create a piece of music. The only acceptable accompaniments are the slight, muffled sounds emanating from the throats of my interlocutors, which indicate, in a minimal and efficient manner (one or two notes should suffice), their comprehension, agreement, surprise, and so on, simply by use of varying intonations.

This is why it is easier (not impossible) to speak a foreign language perfectly, without an accent, that it is the "speak" another culture "without an accent"—without my cultural "accent" putting me in difficulty even if, masked by my linguistic performance, it does not immediately betray my difference. The case of people who have been perfectly bilingual since childhood is interesting in this respect. Thus, X is Franco-American, bilingual and bicultural. It may happen that X, in a conversation in American with Americans, unconsciously adopts the French rhythm and tone of voice. X may then be considered aggressive, quibbling, or noisy by the other conversants, which will surprise and hurt X. Similarly, X, speaking French to French people, might adopt the implicit rules of American conversation without realizing it, and may therefore be considered "slow," "heavy," insistent or dominating, too serious. In both cases, the cultural difference being neither obvious nor even conceivable, X's "fault" is credited to his or her personality. The consequences for X might be more serious if X is unaware of the possible clashes between these two cultures.

In conclusion, I would briefly like to return to language, which seems to summarize the difference between American conversation and French conversation. Centuries ago, "to converse" (*converser*) meant, in French, "to live with someone," "to frequent," a meaning which is still alive in today's French conversation. In American, on the other hand, conversation is "an informal verbal exchange of thoughts," and "to be conversant" means "to know by experience or study," that is to say, "to be a specialist in, good at, exercised in, well informed, capable."

# 3 Parents and Children

"While I was living in France," an American academic told me, "I often saw the following scene: a child does something which his parents don't like, or one of his parents doen't like. The parent tells him to stop. The child continues. Nothing happens, the parents don't say anything and don't do anything. The child continues to do what he was doing. The parents repeat, 'Will you stop that?' and it continues. What good does it do to tell children to stop doing something, if nothing happens when they don't?"

An American student who had just spent the year in France after having made several shorter visits told me, still horrified, about her experience in a Parisian student dorm, which she summarized in these indignant terms: "They treated us like children." What had deeply shocked her was that during one residents' meeting, the director of the dormitory announced that she had gone into the students' rooms while they were away, "because you can learn a lot about people by seeing how they keep their rooms." This particular student shared her room with a French woman and unflinchingly accepted the comings and goings of the maid. It was therefore the fact that the director had entered without permission that seemed an intolerable assault on her private life. In addition, she was surprised that the French students, who were in the majority, did not seem to find this intrusion upsetting or even surprising. Similarly, the nightwatchman treated her "like a little girl" the first time she arrived a quarter of an hour after the curfew at 11 p.m. Not knowing where else to go hardly a month after her arrival in Paris, she insistently banged on the door of the dormitory. The night watchman "lectured her" and "yelled at her." She added this remark which I found surprising: "And he didn't even ask me where I had been; he would have found out that I was coming from the other side of Paris where I had seen a play for a class, and that I had a good reason for being late." The last straw (which convinced her to leave the dormitory) was when the director's assistant ("hardly older than I was") reprimanded her for having forgotten to sign the register upon leaving by making a gesture as if to slap her, while she was "in the presence of an American friend who was in France for the first time" (and who therefore could only interpret the scene from an American perspective).

Americans and the French seem to be in complete agreement on only one point: they do not understand (which means they do not approve of) the way in which the children of "the other culture" are raised. Thus, many "American" situations can be displeasing to a French person. Here are a few, such as they were recounted to me:

—I am engaged in an interesting conversation with X, an American. Just as he is about to answer my question, or else at the most important point in my discourse, his child comes in and interrupts our conversation in what I consider to be an intrusive manner. Instead of teaching him manners, X turns and listens to him. He may even get up, apologize for the interruption by saying that he must give or show something to the little one and that he will return "in a few minutes." X comes back, a smile on his lips, asking, "Where were we?" and resumes the conversation. The worst of it is that if the little child comes back because he didn't find what he was looking for or because something is not working or because he is proud of having finished what he was doing and wants to tell X, he won't hesitate to do so. And X will not hesitate to respond. No doubt about it, these Americans have no manners.

—We're at the dinner table. Y, an American, is sitting next to her three-year-old daughter, who has demanded a setting identical to that of the grown-ups (and received it from the hostess, since the mother seemed to think it was only normal) and is "acting cute." She asks for soup, then refuses to eat it. Her mother is trying to persuade her, saying, "You'll see, it's very good." The little girl finally takes a spoonful, then exclaims, "I hate it, it's yucky." The mother says, "You're going to make Z (the hostess) feel bad," or "No, it's very good," or else (are you ready for this?) "Z's cooking doesn't seem to be a hit with the little one." Slaps, that's what they deserve, these kids! And the parents too, while we're at it! You should see them in restaurants. The kids get up, mosey about, sometimes they even come up to your table to make conversation; they eat like pigs, talk loudly, do whatever they please, as if they were at home; they think they can do anything.

—I'm riding in my car, on the main street of a residential neighborhood. It is not a small, out-of-the-way street that is isolated and quiet, and it certainly is not a dead end. It is a major, busy street. I have to slow down. Right in the middle of the street, on the road, children, yes, children are playing baseball, or with frisbees. They stop, "allow me" to go by with big smiles, sometimes even a little tap on my car. Can't they play elsewhere? This isn't a ghetto—there are big parks nearby, huge lawns surrounding their houses. No, they must have the street, and so they take it, that's all there is to it. They are nice enough to let me go by, why should I complain? You should see how they're dressed, barefoot, right in the middle of the street. These Americans are impossible . . .

The preceding examples represent just a partial collage of comments that I have heard repeatedly concerning American children. And I am sure we (French) can all provide examples, which we have either seen or heard about, concerning their "lack of manners." Spoiled, ill-bred, undisciplined; with no manners, no reserve; egotistical, impolite, constantly moving, running all over, touching everything, making noise . . . Everyone has his favorite story, and not only in France. Many French parents who have been living in the United States for a long time, whose children have been raised in the American style "despite" them, complained about American schools during interviews conducted by my students. "No discipline," "they let them do what they want," "not enough homework," "no general education . . . even I, with the little education I have, know the capital of every country in the world. . . . Go find an American who can tell you that." "No respect," "spoiled rotten," are comments I have often heard and recorded myself. "Here, Madame, it is not the parents who raise their children, it is the children who raise their parents. . . . I'm proud to have remained French. . . . But don't get me wrong, I'm also proud of being an American."

Similarly, Americans have much to say about French children, or rather, perhaps, about French parents. Here is an example told to me by an American, who had obviously been mystified by the scene: "We were having a drink at the house of some friends. She's French (like

my wife), and he's an American (like me). Our children are having
fun together, running in and out of the room, absorbed in chasing
each other. The adults' conversation is suddenly interrupted by G.,
the French lady of the house, who loudly scolds the kids, all the kids,
hers and ours, 'because they're making too much noise and prevent-
ing us from speaking calmly.' This threatening and screaming
happens again—with increasing stridency—each time the children
forget G.'s command in the heat of their chasing. When we get home,
I mention to my wife that G. was the one who had made any conversation nearly impossible with her loud interruptions." He adds, with a
look of amusement, that G. is always complaining about the "rudeness" of Americans, and about the "atrocious" manner in which they
bring up their children ("and in addition she annoys me because she
always says to her husband and me each time she criticizes Americans, 'not you two, of course, you're the exception, we've found the
only two tolerable Americans' . . . but I'm also an American").

Some American students with whom I was studying French magazine advertisements were very impressed by the children's clothing
displayed in certain ads; they admired the interesting colors, the quality of the garments, the style. After a few moments' thought, a few of
them asked, "But how can they play in these clothes?" I sent them to
children's clothing stores, where they could compare the American
clothes with those that had been imported from France, feel them,
study them. To sum up their reactions: they felt that the French
clothes were far prettier but that it was impossible to imagine a child
dressed in them doing anything but standing still or sitting down. It
would be impossible to imagine a child running or roughhousing,
rolling on the ground or even in the grass—in short, playing any game
at which one could get dirty. As far as the baby clothes went, they
noticed something else they found strange: the snaps or other closings
were on the shoulders or at the back of the neck, not between the legs
as on the American clothes. This leads one to believe either that one
undresses the child completely in order to change diapers or that one
doesn't change them very often—which means either that the baby's
comfort comes after his or her appearance or that babies are taught to
control themselves very early. The French clothes were unanimously
condemned, despite their good looks. My students all agreed that a
well-dressed child who must constantly be wary of getting dirty, a
child who thinks about his clothes, is a victimized child.

The opinion of my students on this subject is the same as that of many Americans. Indeed, more than one American has expressed surprise, in my presence, at how French children can remain quiet (*sage*) for hours. Even the expression *être sage*, or *rester sage* makes them smile. It is an expression which is (literally) untranslatable into English (in this case, one would use *well-behaved* which is closer to *qui se conduit bien*). For an American, a child who remains quiet for long periods of times is either sick or, in a sense, oppressed by his parents—parents who restrain his movements, his space, his words, and his freedom. An American would say that he is not a child but a small grown-up.

A scene on the platform at the train station in Rambouillet would seem to confirm the American interpretation. A mother says to her daughter (two or three years old) who is squatting, "Come on, get up. . . . I'll help you walk! . . . Just you wait and see." Then, a few seconds later, "I told you not to mess around like that. . . . Now look how dirty you are. . . . Come on, let me wipe off your hand . . . and then you go and put it in your mouth!" And, as if to prevent her daughter from getting her hands dirty again by touching the ground, she picks her up.

A young American who had spent a year in South of Franch, told me how she had been reprimanded by a little three- or four-year-old French girl in the park. A "teeny-weeny girl" who was passing by, a few steps behind her father, stopped and lectured her on her bare feet, adding that a big girl like her should know better. The father didn't reprimand his daughter. For the American in question, French people "learn to be arrogant" from day one.

And then there are scenes, like the ones described at the beginning of this essay, which evoke the incomprehension or the surprise of the foreigner faced with an unfamiliar situation, a question mark rather than a judgment. Thus the comments of students who have spent some time in French families. One au pair girl said, "When guests were coming for dinner, the parents repeated the rules to the children before the meal." Another one, who took care of a little two-year-old boy in an upper-middle-class family (in a house so large that the children had a separate apartment from their parents, with a remote monitor video camera in their room), said, "I was not supposed to let B. cry, because his father didn't like the noise when they had guests." "When French children are young, the father doesn't pay much attention to them; the children must remain quiet and well-behaved in his presence." "French children do not often sit down just to chat with their parents. One evening, after dinner, I stayed with the parents to talk and watch television. The next morning, their daughter asked me why I had done that." "Madame N. had two sons, a three-year-old and an eight-year-old. The boys always played together, and it was rare to see them with other children. One Sunday, we had a big meal with the entire family. The two boys remained completely still for hours. They didn't say a word at the table. . . . The French demand that a child, even if he is very young, know how to behave himself." "Obedience is very important in French families, the child must respect his parents' wishes and, above all, must not question things. The children are very well-behaved, especially when the father is present. In contrast, when an American child is told to do something by his parents, he often asks "why?" and very often the parents explain why. In the French family, the father is always right." "In the family I lived with, the mother accompanied her daughter to her piano lessons and stayed there during the lessons. She monitored her daughter's progress, even if she had already heard her play a thousand times at home. American children go by themselves to their music or dance lessons, and even if their mothers go with them, they usually don't stay. In the same way, American parents let their children go to school all alone, or else, very often, with friends. In France, I had to bring the children to school and pick them up every day, even if they lived only two minutes away. There was also a crowd of parents who came to pick up their children. They too lived very close to the school." "Parents protect their children in several ways. Outside, their physical movements are restricted: 'Don't run,' 'calm down,' 'slowly,' 'not so loud,' 'don't yell.' In the bookstore, the mother helps her daughter to choose her books. The mother is really the one who chooses them. American children choose their own books." "French children can play all by themselves. . . . When I brought the little girl to the park, she played with her doll all alone, unless her brother was there, in which case, before going to play with her brother, she liked to say to her doll 'don't get dirty, you hear' in imitation of her mother." "My friend's children were five, ten, and thirteen, but they had no problem in playing together. American children, on the other hand, don't like playing with their little brothers or sisters." "It is not uncommon to see a parent slap his child in public. . . . American parents wait to get home to punish their children, because it is very important that the child not be ridiculed in front of his friends."

This final sentence explains why the American who had told me of her experience in a student dormitory was so annoyed at having been reprimanded, even gently, in front of her American friend who was in France for the first time. She considered herself to be an adult and was treated like a child, and in the cruelest fashion to boot: ridiculed in front of a friend.

I cannot go into all the cases that I collected. But if there were any doubts as to the differences between the French and the Americans in the realm of parent-child relationships, I think that the preceding pages will have sufficed to eliminate them. The analysis of these first-hand reports, of my interviews and observations, helped me become aware of the distance separating the cultural premises informing these relationships.

A French woman told me, to show her joy and approval on the day of her daughter's second marriage; "For me, it's the first time she's marrying," thereby erasing, in one fell swoop, the seven years of her daughter's life which had been dedicated to her first marriage and the first husband, whom—as she was aware—I knew well. Only the second marriage counted for her (as she told all the guests) not only, I think, because she liked and approved of the second husband very much, but also, and especially, I believe, because her daughter, who until then had refused maternity, was expecting a baby and was radiant with joy. In her eyes, her daughter had finally reached maturity. During the intimate reception which followed the ceremony, the mother expressed concern more than once about her daughter's health, insisting that she sit down and rest. The other members of her family, and of her husband's family, were doing the same. My young friend's nice round belly no longer seemed to belong to her. She had suddenly become the repository of a being over whom both families had rights.

Getting married or living together is already a social act, of course, inasmuch as it consists of presenting oneself, if only to one's closest friends and family, as someone's partner in a permanent association (even if it later turns out to be temporary). But neither the family nor society acquires rights over the partner in question. As soon as two people become parents, however, they are expected to become "good parents," under the surveillance of many vigilant eyes. To bring a child into the world is therefore an eminently social act in France. It is easier to understand, in this context, why many French feminists sang the praises of childbirth as self-discovery, as physical joy, as intimately personal, as egotistical. What seems to be a contradiction to American feminists (a feminist expressing joy at being a mother) becomes easily understandable once we see that these women are reclaiming the experience of childbirth for themselves, which goes against the implicit definition of childbirth as a social act.

Indeed, as soon as I become a parent in France, I must answer to society for my behavior toward the child. As a parent, my role is to transform this "malleable, innocent, impressionable, and irresponsible" creature into a social being, a responsible member of the society, which is prepared to integrate him or her in exchange for a pledge of allegiance. This means that on becoming a parent, it is first and foremost to the society that I incur an obligation, a debt, rather than to my child, who comes second. If I give priority to my child, I isolate myself from this society.

A child is therefore a link between his parents and society—others, people in general, whoever is outside of the father-mother-child triangle; and even within this triangle, whoever, at any moment is outside of the relationship between one parent (mother or father) and the child. In other words, my behavior with respect to my child is constantly subject to the judgment of others, which explains why I am always tempted to justify myself when my child's conduct does not correspond, or might not correspond, to what a third party, even someone totally unknown to me, might expect. If my child "behaves badly," therefore, I am immediately placed in a conflictful situation: I must show others that I know the rules and that I am wearing myself out trying to teach them to my child; at the same time, I must show my child that I love him or her anyway, that the bond between us cannot be destroyed so easily, since it is precisely because of this given of parental love that the child will attempt to change, to improve the conduct that displeases me so because it displeases others. This could even lead me, as a parent, to create a perfect double-bind: "You are not my daughter any more" or "You are not my son any more." As a matter of fact, this threat, which is quite common, can have meaning and thereby bring about results only insofar as it contains its own negation. Indeed, if by saying "You are not my child any more" I were confirming a real rupture, as when I say "You are not my friend any more" or "You are no longer my lover," my child would have no reason to behave differently in order to please me. It is because I, and (French) society, have established my love as noncontingent and the ties that bind us as indestructible, even if we no longer want them, that my threat can have an effect. My child and I know, implicitly, that what I am saying is: "You are behaving yourself in a way that shames me, that makes me feel bad, that hurts me. You are not behaving like the perfect child worthy of my love. Other people's disapproval of your conduct is a reflection on me."

From this perspective, it becomes apparent that the constant commands at the table ("Don't put your elbows on the table," "Sit up straight," "Don't talk with your mouth full," etc.), the scolding in cafés, the "bawling out" in the street, the quick spanking or slap just about anywhere, the lecture, or even, simply, the reproving gesture or look, all fall into a single category. It is less a matter of showing my anger, which would be impolite since I must remain in control of myself in public (hence the "wait till we get home . . ."), than it is of showing others the efforts I am making to bring up my child correctly. In other words, by scolding, slapping, and repeating "Are you going to stop that?" I am justifying myself in the eyes of others. If my child behaves poorly, it is not my fault, I've done everything I could to make things different. I am a "good parent," but I have to fight against the nature of children ("You know how kids are") or, even worse, against "bad influences." The older my child gets, the more the "bad influences" will be responsible for his deviant behavior, and certainly for all criminal conduct. (Question: Are there parents who prevent their children from having a bad influence on their friends?)

The pressure must be very strong for it to maintain such a hold over parents. It is. We are all familiar with the reproving glances that converge upon parents who "don't know how to control their child." If these glances have no effect, bystanders turn to each other with gestures of disapproval for the "guilty parents" and finally resort to making comments indirectly addressed to the parents. In an extreme case, if the parents remain oblivious to even the most clearly expressed reprobation, it is not unusual to see others intervene directly, as often happens at the beach ("It isn't nice to throw sand on people," "If I catch you . . ."). Moreover, in the absence of parents—in the neighborhood, in the street, and so on—neighbors feel invested with parental responsibility with respect to all the children they know and even those they don't ("If your mother (father) could see you . . ."). A little scene, which I very recently witnessed in Paris, illustrates this perfectly. A waiting room, filled with various families. It is a long wait, people are getting impatient, children are running around, but in what is still a "tolerable" fashion. One little boy has obviously gone too far, as a grandmother, who is part of our group, tells me: "There was a little boy who was kicking his grandmother, so I caught him and told him, 'You're tired, aren't you, I'm sure you didn't mean to kick your grandmother, but you're very tired. Now be a good little boy and go ask your grandmother to forgive you.' Really, I wouldn't want to be his grandmother." The woman who told me this seemed satisfied and rather proud of her action (she told me about it several times), of having put the little boy on the right track. I think she would have been scandalized if I had told her even in a polite manner that "she should mind her own business" or that she had assumed rights that in no way were hers, which would probably have been the American interpretation of the scene.

This assumption of responsibility works both ways. A child by himself (or with other children) who is crying will be consoled, protected, helped, and reassured by a passing adult. Thus, on the whole, all adults are responsible for all children, and, within this group, certain adults have the exclusive care of certain children, their own, but on condition that they "pass the test" to which they are constantly subjected by any member of the group.

To understand the American situation, one need only in a sense reverse all the signs. Of course, in this case too, the parents take responsibility for the education of their children. But the essential difference is that this responsibility is theirs alone. When I (an American) become a parent, I incur an obligation to my children rather than to society, which comes second. My obligation is not to teach my children the rules and practices of society, but above all to give them every possible chance to discover and develop their "natural qualities," to exploit their gifts, and to blossom.

Thus, when I raise my child in the French style, in a sense what I am doing is clearing a patch of ground, pulling out the weeds, cutting, planting, and so on, in order to make a beautiful garden which will be in perfect harmony with the other gardens. This means that I have in mind a clear idea of the results I want to obtain, and of what I must do to obtain them. My only difficulty will lie in the nature of the soil, given that I apply myself regularly to the task, that is. But when I raise my child American-style, it is almost as if I were planting a seed in the ground without knowing for sure what type of seed it was. I must devote myself to giving it food, air, space, light, a supporting stake if necessary, care, water—in short, all that the seed needs to develop as best it can. And then I wait, I follow the developments closely, I attend to any needs what may arise, and I try to guess what type of plant it will be. I can hope for the best, of course. But if I try to give shape to my dreams, to transform my tomato seed into a potato, for example, I am not a "good parent." To be a good parent, I must therefore give my children every chance, every "opportunity" possible, and then "let nature take its course." If I teach them good manners and social practices, it is to give them an additional chance, knowing that they will need these things to "succeed" in life, to fulfill themselves—that music, dance, and sports lessons, books, toys and all types of gadgets, will favor their development. Once I have assured them a "higher education," that is to say, four years of study at the universities of their choice, I will have done everything possible to give them the best means to realize all their dreams, to choose who and what they want to be.

In other words, it is the French parents who are put to the test; their role as spokespersons for society and their performance as teachers are evaluated. But it is the American children who are put to the test; it is up to them to show their parents what they can do with the chances that have been given them; up to them to prove that they haven't wasted these chances but made maximum use of them; up to them to satisfy the hopes their parents have blindly placed in them.

From this perspective, it becomes clear that French childhood is an apprenticeship, during which one learns the rules and acquires "good habits"; it is a time of discipline, of imitation of models, of preparation for the role of adult. As one French informant told me, "we had a lot of homework to do and little time to play." American childhood is, on the contrary, a period of great freedom, of games, of experimentation and exploration, during which restrictions are only imposed when there is a serious threat of danger.

In the same vein, American parents avoid as much as possible criticizing their children, making fun of their tastes, or telling them constantly "how to do things." French parents, on the other hand, train their children to "defend themselves well," verbally that is.

Thus, by ordering the child "not to speak if he has nothing to say," "not to act cute," or "not to say silly things," I force her or him to discover the best ways of retaining my attention. According to an American informant, "In France, if the child has something to say, others listen to him. But the child can't take too much time and still retain his audience; if he delays, the family finishes his sentences for him. This gets him in the habit of formulating his ideas better before he speaks. Children learn to speak quickly, and to be interesting." To be amusing as well. That is to say, the child is encouraged to imitate adults but not to copy them "like a parrot." The implicit message is "do like me, but differently." While teaching my child the rules by criticizing or making fun of him or her ("you're really going out like that?"; "you look ridiculous in those clothes"; "Come on, you're joking; you couldn't be going out dressed like that"; "A green shirt and red shorts? Sure . . . going to the circus?"; I force him or her at the same time to break free of me by affirming very definite tastes and well-formed opinions.

An American parent will try to do exactly the opposite. As an "ideal" parent, I will patiently listen to all that my child wants to tell me without interrupting, I will compliment him or her for having dressed without assistance (in the beginning), with no comment on the strange assortment he or she has chosen. Later, I will allow my child to buy the clothes he or she chooses, even if they make my hair stand on end, if my suggestions ("don't you think that . . .") have been rejected. The most important thing here, as in all the games we play together, is to give children plenty of room to make their own mistakes and to find their own solutions.

When a child reaches adolescence (the exact age is unimportant, let's just say that it represents the period between childhood and adulthood), the situation seems to reverse itself. For French children, the prize for this long apprenticeship, for these years of obedience and good conduct, is the freedom to do what they want, that is, to stay out late, to "have a good time," maybe to get drunk, to have sexual experiences, to travel, and so on. Even if their parents continue their roles as educators and critics, deep down they recognize the adolescents' right to "do exactly as they please," or at least they resign themselves to this ("youth must have its fling"). The fact that the adolescent continues to be fed, housed, and clothed by his or her parents in no way affects his or her "independence": I am independent if I know what I want and do what I want no matter how things look from the outside. It is therefore possible for my parents to continue to remonstrate with me, to "give me orders," or to advise me; I may grow impatient with this, but it is essentially unimportant, since I can always let them "say what they want," let them play their roles, without it producing any greater change in my behavior than a nominal acquiescence. Thus, in the student dormitory described by the American earlier, it is likely that the French students weren't bothered by the director's inspection of their rooms, the assistant's remonstrances, or the night watchman's yelling and lecturing because all that corresponded to the quasi-parental roles that these people in charge were supposed to assume, and all one had to do was let them play their roles in order to be "left in peace." On the other hand, it seems to me that a French student would have found any questions from the night watchman concerning her arrival at the dormitory after the curfew out of place (and would have refused to answer them), whereas the American student regretted the fact that he had accused her without giving her the opportunity to explain her lateness and justify it.

American adolescents insist more on the exterior signs of independence. The first sign will be economic: very early on, they will show that they can earn money and "take care of themselves," that is, pay for everything they would consider it "childish" to expect parents to pay for (records, a stereo, sporting equipment, a motor bike, etc.). This is often interpreted by French people as indisputable proof of the "well-known American materialism." In fact, what young Americans are doing, is, on the contrary, proving that they are capable of taking care of themselves, showing that they are capable of putting to good use the chances their parents made every effort (to the point of sacrifice) to give them. The second exterior sign of independence is affective: it is important to "leave home," even if one gets along marvelously with one's parents, if only to reassure them. American parents worry if their children hesitate to "stand on their own two feet," if they give what parents interpret as signs of "dependency," of "insecurity," of an "unhealthy" need for protection, or if they "act like children." This means that even if, deep down, I (an American) think that my child is still immature, it is important that the outward signs I give to the child show the opposite, not because I am a hypocrite but because I am convinced that it will help him or her to reach maturity. And it is even more important that I do this in the presence of others—in the presence of my child's friends as well as in the presence of mine.

In exchange, all my children's "successes" belong to them alone. I can go to all their tennis matches, or anxiously attend their concerts, but I would indignantly reject the slightest suggestion that they owe their success to me in any way. I only gave them the chance.

Since Americans "do what they want," in a sense, from childhood, it is much less important for them to "know" what they want very early on. Parents accept, if they do not encourage, having their children "experience different lifestyles," hesitate between careers—in short, not "settle down too soon," which could reduce their chances and restrict their potential (which explains why most programs of univer- sity study, including law and medicine, include four preliminary years of college). The weight of these maximum opportunities given to young Americans puts very strong pressure on them, early on, to "prove themselves," to show their parents (and the world) what they are capable of. But since the expectations have never been clearly defined, and ideally cannot be so, logically there can be no moment when the goal is reached. The implicit parental injunction is to always seize every opportunity, to climb farther and higher, without rest, to always be "on the go." Not to do so is to condemn oneself to medi- ocrity, to wasted chances, to the ultimate failure which consists of not exploiting one's human potential to the fullest.

One of the consequences of all of the above is that the majority of French people interviewed have better memories of their adolescence ("it was sheer madness") than of their childhood, happy as it may have been. Childhood is full of restrictions: adolescence is, or is recon- structed in retrospect to be, a burst of freedom, memorable exper- iences with friends, a kind of happy interlude. One can let loose and kid around, have an attack of the giggles, or play "practical jokes," which Americans of the same age have trouble understanding, be- cause for them these are the hallmarks of childish behavior.

In contrast, when Americans reach adolescence, they are suddenly confronted with all sorts of expectations, real or imagined; they are expected to take on responsibilities and to perform. It is time for them to take their places on a stage from which they will no longer step down without a profound sense of failure. Hence the nervousness, the panic which often seizes American adolescents when they must say goodbye to the total freedom, the games and carefree attitude of their childhood world. For the majority of Americans, childhood becomes a paradise lost. Whether or not I had a happy childhood is irrelevant; if I hadn't, it means that I was cheated twice: cheated of my right to "opportunities" and cheated of my right to a few years of paradise, to that blessed time when I neither had to be an adult nor pretend to be one.

Thus, whereas young Americans do not understand why young French people often "act like children," young French people in the United States often remark that young Americans are "too serious," that they "don't know how to have fun," that they "give boring parties," in short, that they "act like adults."

These differences between young American and French people, this systematic inversion of the signs, so to speak, between the two systems, are also found in the relationships between children and adults in the two cultures.

While French parents educate their children, they cannot, at the same time, be their playmates, save in exceptional circumstances when the rules arc, so to speak, suspended. And in this case, the parent plays at being a child, thus putting him- or herself on the same level as the child. Whenever he or she wants to play, the French child turns to the other children in the family, no matter what their ages, and is heartily encouraged by his or her parents to do so. He or she is also encouraged to serve as a replacement for the parents when with the younger children, at school and in the street. Parents reinforce this solidarity between the children by refusing to intervene in case of a dispute. In the words of one informant, "When I went to my mother, I got an extra smack . . . so it didn't take me long to learn." It is therefore up to the children to "work things out among themselves." And never, never should they come and "tell"; this is definitely not a way of getting on the parents' good side, but quite the contrary. Little by little, this system teaches children to stick together against parental authority. And this relationship is reproduced at school. At the same time, within the family structure, each parent establishes an independent relationship with each child, and each child does the same with his or her brothers and sisters. Each family member is therefore engaged in a network of independent relationships and is witness to (or judge of) the relationships between each family member and the others. In the case of an argument between two family members, this allows a third, who is uninvolved in the dispute, to play the role of the go-between, to interpret one's behavior for the other ("You know, you have to understand your father"; "You know, your mother is very tired these days"; "Don't get angry, he's studying for finals and is very nervous"). The child therefore gets used to a multitude of simultaneous relationships and to the presence of intermediaries, of go-betweens.

The role played by the intermediary in "arranging the situation" explains why a parent's intervention at school and, as we shall see, at the university is accepted or at least tolerated by French children, whereas it would be unacceptable if not unbearable to American children. Thus, a French couple, in France, asked me to explain the higher education system in the United States because their son wanted to go there. Both of them were educated and "modern." I explained. Armed with my experience of frequent cultural misunderstandings, I was preparing to discuss what I consider to be most important, that is to say, the expectations to which French people would not be accustomed. To illustrate this, I began to tell a story that some (French) friends had just told me, about how they had furiously intervened at the *grande école* (a unique French institution) because their son, it seems, had been slighted by the "incompetence" of some of its staff. I was about to say that this type of thing could not happen in the United States or would be considered very inappropriate (by the son himself, who would feel he was being taken charge of "like a child") when, fortunately for the relationship between the couple and myself, I was interrupted by the mother who said, "Oh, yes, it's like Alain," and told me, indignantly, about all of her protests at the medical school in which her son was enrolled concerning the "stupid" aggravation they had given him. I immediately stopped talking, experiencing the dizzy sensation one feels at the edge of a cliff.

American children are encouraged very early on to play with other children their own age (and therefore outside of the family), to "make friends," to learn to establish relationships with strangers, to "become popular" among their peers. At home, they seek the approval or encouragement (and, hopefully, some day, admiration) of their parents; it is therefore only logical that they feel in competition with their brothers and sisters. The same thing happens at school: they must both make friends among their classmates and compete with them for the attention and approval of teachers, and later on of professors, for whom they will "do the best they can." This competition is not meant to be destructive; rather it aims to stimulate children, to extract or elicit the best possible performance from each one, and "may the best one win." And like the parent, the teacher will not allow him- or herself to criticize a student's work in public, but will give the student the means to find and develop the area he or she can excel in. A teacher who makes curt, scornful, or even joking comments about each paper he or she returns, as would be possible in the French system, might be considered sick or deranged—in any case, inept at teaching. The class would simply be deserted, as I've seen happen in an American university to a young instructor right off the boat from France. The American student, accustomed since childhood to explanations rather than to pronouncements or encouragements to emulate, does not hesitate to ask questions, to discuss, to disagree, to question—behavior which always surprises French students visiting the United States. What surprises them even more is that the professor does not take the question as a sign of hostility, a challenge to his or her authority, but treats it as a sign of intellectual independence, or a sincere desire to better understand the question or to participate in the discussion of a subject that interests her or him—an attitude which a "good" professor will seek to encourage. We should note here that American students spontaneously turn to the professor rather than to their classmates, thereby recreating the relationship they have established with their parents. The relationship is of concern only to two people. No one has the right to intervene, to "interfere" in this relationship, not even, in the family, the other parent.

For the young French person, then, reaching maturity consists of assuming the role for which my parents and other educators have prepared me, that of being an "educator" (in the broadest sense) in turn, of taking my place and taking on my responsibilities in society, and beginning the cycle all over again. Whatever my age, though, my conduct will always be a reflection on my parents, who share my successes as well as my disappointments. At this time, I will also begin to attend to my parents' well-being and will tacitly commit myself to taking care of them in their old age, to reversing the roles. I will, in turn, be judged, by whoever feels it is his right, on the way in which I treat my parents.

For an American, maturity is a much more fluid concept which varies from person to person. I can, therefore, be a responsible adult (I have a permanent job, a house, a family, I pay my bills and taxes) and still be considered immature by certain people, whereas others will envy the fact that I have retained a certain "childlike" side (a taste for taking risks, a capacity for wonderment and amazement, a refusal to accept the impossible, etc.). In the end, I alone decide if I have reached maturity or not. And just as my parents always went out of their way to allow me to be responsible for myself, often at the price of a strict control on their desires to do otherwise, so I will not treat my old parents as children by inflicting on them the "indignity" of taking care of them (at my home) but will make certain of the security and comfort of their environment and of the possibility of their having a "social life" with people whose company they appreciate, that is to say, people their own age. My family and I will visit them, but they have earned the right to have a quiet or fast-paced life, as they choose, in any case a life free of the demands and tears of small children. For a French person, however, this means that Americans "abandon" their aged parents.

Faced with such profound cultural differences at practically each stage in the life cycle, we can only marvel, not at the number of sources for misunderstandings, but rather at the possibilities for—and the existence of—any understandings at all.

# 4   The Couple

Following a paper on intercultural misunderstandings which I presented at a conference in France, a French colleague waited at the door to tell me that she "totally agreed" with everything I had said, and in particular with what I had said about intercultural couples. "I'm in the process of getting a divorce, you see. My husband is American, and he does everything exactly as you said, and it gets on my nerves . . . and I'm sure I get on his nerves as well, because I also do everything you said. . . . We finally realized that it couldn't work out."

A Frenchman who had been married to an American for several years said, "I love my wife . . . but she will always be an intimate stranger to me." An American woman who had lived with a Frenchman summarized her experience in these terms: "If I had wanted to have a child, I would have liked to have it with him, but never in a million years would I have wanted him to be the father of my child." Thus, in a single sentence, she had managed to separate the genetic being from the cultural being. A young Frenchman in the United States: "I had an American girlfriend whom I liked very much; we got along very well, but it couldn't work out: she wanted me to call before coming to see her, in case she was busy or had too much work. . . . I ended up breaking up with her; if I can't stop by to see my girlfriend when I feel like it, what's the use?" An American woman after a year in France: "I left a note on my door for Henri, telling him to leave me a note if he wanted to go out that evening. . . . We didn't have a telephone and it was difficult to communicate. . . . When I came back, my note was no longer there, but Henri hadn't left a note; I went out. . . . I didn't see Henri again for three days. . . . He was angry because I wasn't there when he came to see me." Another woman said, "I had many problems with Jacques. He always said he loved me, but when we went out we were rarely alone, we were always with his friends."

The same message comes through on both sides: a difference which is attractive, then baffling. Sometimes, these small difficulties accumulate and transform themselves into "couples' problems," leading to a breakup or even a divorce. Since the problems specific to couples are routinely studied and treated on both sides of the Atlantic, no one is surprised to hear about them. Just another case of incompatibility, people say.

It is possible (and even probable) that the breakups of many heterocultural couples are due to problems of incompatibility identical to those of homocultural couples. I am, however, convinced that differences in cultural premises are at the root of much of the pain that these heterocultural couples experience—pain that we have a hard time forgetting or forgiving, the more so as we do not understand it. We can, in effect, know that we are different, without knowing exactly how this difference functions. In other words, I am well aware that there may exist as many ways of making love as there are cultures. But of loving?

As the previous sentence suggests, we become a couple because we love each other: this is already a cultural presupposition, but one which is common to French and American cultures. This situation is different from that of "marriage"—a word which, in French, is often used in association with another word defining its nature (*mariage d'argent*, "for money"; *mariage de convenance*, for "social reasons"; *mariage de raison*, "arranged marriage"; and finally *mariage d'amour*, "for love") whereas in American, although these categories exist, they are not referred to in the same manner. In American, the word "marriage" seems to presuppose the (vague) notion of "love," since in everyday language, it is qualified only by terms like "traditional" or "open," as well as "happy/unhappy," and so on. It is only when it is not a marriage for "love" that one must specify: "He (or she or they) married for money (or power, etc.)."

Let's get back to the couple. If I say, whether in French or in English, "we were three couples at dinner last night," this supposes three men and three women, that is to say, heterosexual couples. If, in fact, I counted a homosexual couple among these three couples, I will have to suggest this in the course of conversation (by giving their names, for example) because the language still forces me to specify "homosexual" and continues to treat "heterosexual" as redundant (as the "unmarked category").

In both cultures, therefore, the couple is by definition heterosexual. It involves a man and woman who are married, or as good as married, and whom we assume to be united by sexual bonds. In the singular, the term suggests a certain permanence, a kind of legitimacy as well as exclusivity in a sexual relationship (as opposed to "lovers," for example). It is strange to note that in the plural, the term evokes only the sketchy promise or possibility of ties, as when we speak of couples who come together and break apart in dance. It is similarities like those I have just mentioned that, unbeknownst to us, often lead us into errors and prevent us from becoming aware of the profound differences between the two cultures concerning the meaning of the couple.

In French, when I think of a "couple," two expressions come immediately to mind, *assorti* or *mal assorti* ("likely" and "unlikely"—literally "matched" and "mismatched"). It even seems to me that one makes this association automatically, when one wants to describe a certain couple to someone else. What we should note here is that the assertion "they make a likely (an unlikely) couple" is sufficient and needs no qualification, modification, or clarification. This presupposes, therefore, that my interlocutor and I immediately understand the implications and that we may not need to go any further with the description. This means, in fact, that this definition is a judgment of the couple based on exterior characteristics, on signs considered to be evident and unequivocal. An unlikely couple will exhibit differences which we (French) find too great in the following categories: physical appearance (tall/short, fat/thin, beautiful [handsome]/ugly, robust/puny); age; social class, to the extent that it is betrayed by their clothing (good/poor quality, discreet/ostentatious, elegant/gaudy); and behavior (correct/out of place). Personality differences only come into play if they are visible (nervous/calm, for example). Otherwise, if I speak about the "matched" or "mismatched" personalities of the two partners, I am affirming that I know the couple better than just "by sight." This exterior definition of the couple suggests that we all have a composite portrait of the perfect couple in our minds, upon which we (the French) would all agree. This exterior description of the couple has such power that it is not unusual for me to use it when speaking about the very couple of which I am a part ("we make a very/ rather/not at all likely couple").

Thus, "the couple" is a social category (for the French). It is the affirmation of certain social values: to be part of a couple is to proclaim sexual bonds that are approved, made legal, legitimate, or licit by marriage, living together, or simply by the tacit, public approval of social as well as sexual ties. Forming a couple is a social act, unlike having a lover. Indeed, needless to say, forming a couple is different from coupling. This means that in order to exist, my couple relationship must be "spoken": we put others in the habit of combining our names by doing so ourselves, by our discourse in front of others, and by our behavior in the presence of others.

Indeed, once I present my association with a partner as a couple relationship, I actualize what might seem contradictory: just as I confirm real or possible sexual bonds (as opposed to the bonds of family, friendship, or business, for example), I suppress anything that might suggest the existence of these bonds from my behavior. That is to say, our behavior as a couple will be different, depending on whether we are in the presence of others. The distinction between these two types of conduct recreates, in a sense, the rigorous separation that exists in France between the house and street and, inside the house, between the accessible rooms and the rooms that are off-limits (see the chapter on the home). This distinction allows for no gray area. Thus, the couple "at home," but in front of the open window or within earshot of others, must, or at least should, behave as in public.

At home, "inside," with no witnesses, we have intimacy, separation from others, sexuality. Behind the walls of the house, the couple's intimate behavior is of concern only to themselves; further, the couple should not "make a spectacle of themselves" if they do not want to be accused of exhibitionism. If the members of the couple become "parents," the presence of these intimate witnesses (the children) will affect their "sexual" conduct, if not their sexual discourse. Unless I am admitted to the intimacy of a couple, I will only know this couple by their "outside" conduct, their social conduct. In this context, all that brings the two partners together exclusively is suddenly forbidden; all that isolates them from the group, all that is unduly reminiscent of the other relationship, that of the "inside," is forbidden. (Thus, according to the rules in a guide to good manners, "it is best not to use the term *mon chéri*—'my love'—too much in public; terms like 'pussycat,' 'sweetheart,' and 'angel' should be reserved for intimate settings.") "Tenderness" is allowed, but anything "passionate" becomes practically taboo in public. It seems paradoxical that a French couple never behaves "in public" like people "in love" or "lovers," who "live for each other." This means that if X (whom I know well, and who therefore knows that I am part of a couple) sees me on the street with Y, whom X does not know, X can conclude that Y is my lover only if we behave in a manner that couples should reserve for "inside" (that is, if we "advertise" our relationship); indeed, if X, who knows that I am part of a couple with W, sees me with Y and our conduct suggests no "illicit" behavior, X will probably assume that Y and I are buddies, colleagues, or friends. But if I meet X, whom I have not seen in a while (he therefore may not be up on my love life), and he sees me with Z, he has no way of knowing if Z is one of my friends, my husband, or the person I live with if I do not make it clear whether we are a couple or friends (for instance, there is nothing wrong with walking arm in arm with a friend).

Let's go back to the "problems" that the American mentioned at the beginning of this essay said she had with "Jacques": "He always said he loved me, but when we went out, we were rarely alone, we were always with his friends." Another American told me of the difficulty she had in understanding a similar experience: "I ate every day with Gérard at the student restaurant. If his friends were there, we had to sit at their table; if Gérard was with them, he always sat at the end, and a seat was reserved at the end for me as well. His friends didn't speak to me. If his friends arrived and Gérard and I were already there, they went to sit elsewhere, even if there was room left at our table, then came over to say hello later. . . . I think they just didn't like me. . . . One time, we were at a party and everyone was dancing, and all of Gérard's friends asked me to dance, and kept me from dancing with Gérard all evening . . . and Gérard was laughing. . . . I really didn't get it, and I was very hurt. . . . He was so different when we were alone."

Whatever the personalities of Gérard and his friends, it seems possible to interpret their behavior in the light of what we have just seen concerning the couple and "intimacy"; others will not come and disturb them, will not act as a "fifth wheel," if a couple is already closed onto themselves (sitting at a table face to face, for example); but if they join the group, the gang, friends, or family, the group has priority over the couple and does not admit an exclusive relationship. Of course, the group's tolerance changes according to the age of its members, the circumstances, and so on, but the fact remains that if I want to be a part of my group, I must not deny its presence by acting as if it were not there. In exchange, the group will tolerate my partner and will submit him or her to all sorts of little games to put him or her to the test (as, for example, systematically separating us by inviting me or the other person to dance) before being able to consider admitting her or him. In other words, the group must make sure that my couple relationship does not affect or threaten my other relationships—those with my friends, my family, and so on. If we live together, "sexual" behavior, that is, behavior which excludes others (long passionate kisses, caressing each other) is even less admissible ("Hey, come on, why don't you just go home . . .") and is clearly interpreted as antisocial.

While the French couple must behave in a "decent" fashion in front of all those with whom one of the two has already established ties, they are not subjected to such severe restrictions in front of strangers. I can therefore recognize or deny (reject) the presence of others, recognize or deny the bonds that unite us, simply by the way I behave with my partner in front of them. Hence the great variety in the public conduct of French couples (which sometimes offends foreigners).

I believe it is possible to show with words what I have less freedom to show with gestures (with my body): the bonds uniting my partner and myself. It is not the number of "dears" that will be telling but rather the nature of the discourse that I allow myself (and him or her) to carry on. When we are with others, in the presence of friends, my partner and I can gently poke fun at each other, as well as joke or make quips about each other ("attack each other," according to an American interpretation). We can contradict each other, have "violent" discussions, or take opposing sides on an issue. We can "intervene" ("Wouldn't you be better off not having another drink? You know how bad it is for you"; "Don't get so excited, you'll have a heart attack"; "No, he's just kidding, he's not angry at all"), or be extremely attentive ("You're not too tired?"; "You're sure you don't mind?"); we can become exasperated with each other ("Oh, you always exaggerate") and even get angry without worring our friends in the least; on the contrary ("Oh, they've always been that way," or else "They fight from morning to night, but they couldn't live without each other"). In fact, I would go so far as to say that one would probably be wary of a couple who always seemed to be in perfect agreement; people would probably begin to worry and to suspect that there was "something wrong," that "something was fishy." And in the end one might be even somewhat sickened at their being (or having become) "rather boring."

All this would seem profoundly shocking to an American. Indeed, it is by publicly reducing the space between us, by the gestures and physical contact which I (as an American) allow my partner, that I show that we form a couple. This explains why Americans are shocked when they see French women arm in arm, or Frenchmen kissing on the cheeks (to say goodbye for example). I will always remember the sudden rigidity which invaded the until then relaxed bodies of several American friends when a French anthropologist, who had been very happy with his visit, kissed everyone goodbye at the airport. On the other hand, a young American, who "knew that French people kiss all the time to say hello and goodbye," almost unknowingly found himself involved in a homosexual adventure shortly after his arrival in France.

Paradoxically, the potentially sexual nature of the couple is denied in the United States at the same time that the formation of couples is encouraged very early on by the dating system: an eleven-, twelve-, or thirteen-year-old boy and girl go the movies together (often a parent drops them off and picks them up), to a party (birthday or other), or to a sporting match. If they "go out" regularly together, it means they are "going steady," which is to say that they represent a kind of "mini-couple," the nonsexual nature of which is guaranteed (as far as possible) by the adult injunction "not to do anything," by chaperons at dances and other school activities, and by the discreet surveillance permitted the parent who acts as chauffeur. The nearness of bodies therefore indicates not a sexual relationship but rather that a sexual relationship would eventually be permitted between these two people. The logical consequence of this premise is that I (an American) will carefully control the space that separates me from others and the nature of our contact. (Thus, a slap on the back is an acceptable contact between two men; similarly, football players can pat each other's buttocks or throw themselves into each others' arms because this contact, which is taboo anywhere but on athletic fields, is clearly defined as nonsexual by the unambiguously "masculine" context of football.)

It is therefore easy for an American to pick out "couples" on the street: two people of the opposite sex, or of the same sex, who are holding hands, are very close to one another, are arm in arm, have one's head on the other's shoulder, or are simply looking at each other while walking. Further, I will allow this type of contact only with the person I accept as a real or potential sexual partner. Hence the incomprehension of French people, who interpret what is merely a signaling system as "puritan prudery." Unlike French people who must "speak" their couple relationship, I (an American) affirm mine by the visual image I give; by leaving no space between my partner and myself, I present us as a social unit. My friends will expect to see us together "all the time," and they will invite us together, as a couple. Even our relatives will invite us as a couple (to a restaurant, a concert, a picnic, a party). Not inviting my partner is a refusal, a rejection, of me, and I will therefore not accept the invitation; hence the frequent familial difficulties when my relatives do not treat my partner and myself as "inseparable."

We (Americans) can accept unlikely couples, those who display differences (which corresponds to the French *mal assorti*), but it is difficult if not impossible for us to consider two people who are not manifestly united as a "real couple," a "good couple." This unity-union is visible in their way of looking happy together, in their smiles, and in the interest they show in one another. More than anything, it is through and in their discourse that they are going to express this unity: the ideal American couple always agrees. No contradictions, and especially no "corrections" ("No, Gus isn't the one who said that, Al did"), no admonition, no intervention, no advice, no disagreement, no radically different opinions, no fighting, no frowns, no disapproving silences, no reproahces, no anger, and especially, especially, no yelling. All conflict, all threat of conflict or suggestion of conflict, is a bad sign: the couple has "problems" and probably will not last.

But the absence of conflict is not enough: there has to be manifest support of the other, which must constantly be reaffirmed. If my companion is attacked, I must immediately defend him or her, take his or her side, explain why the attack is unjustified. I must not say bad things about her to others, in her presence or in her absence. I must encourage him in his wildest undertakings, even if I am the only one to do so, if the undertaking will make him happy ("He was very supportive"; "She supported me through it all"). And I do this not so much for onlookers, for others, as for my partner, to show him or her my love. In order to prove my love completely, I must support him without reserve or hesitation, as is obvious in my good mood and my smiling face.

Similarly, all physical separation threatens the couple. This is why Americans have trouble understanding the style of many French family vacations, where the wife leaves first with the children for the beach or the mountains, is joined by her husband during his vacation, and often remains behind with the children after the husband has returned to work. In a pinch, forced, inevitable separations (because of work, familial problems, etc.) are okay; but voluntary separations? People will be doubtful; is the couple really functioning well?

Here we must understand that the fact that partners should agree is a presupposition in the formation of the couple, a cultural premise. This means that if there is a conflict in my relationship, I myself (an American) will think that something is wrong and will do my best to understand where the source of this discord lies and how I can make it disappear. That I try hard to do this is not a sign of hypocrisy but, on the contrary, of my good intentions. In fact I judge my own relationship ("it works" or "it doesn't work") as others would, by using the same clues, which means that there can be no difference between public and private conduct, that one is a prolongation of the other. Consequently, it is not unusual for even the children of a divorcing couple to be very surprised by the news ("I never saw my parents argue"; "They always agreed"). In such a case, French people would tend to accuse the couple of hypocrisy, of "disguising the truth", which would, as we see, be an ethnocentric interpretation. Similarly, many Americans told me they were surprised at how "French couples quarrel, bicker all the time over nothing," thereby giving an ethnocentric interpretation, in turn, of relations considered not only acceptable but maybe even desirable by French couples.

I was witness to an incalculable number of misunderstandings of the type I have described, even to the slow disintegration of a Franco-

American relationship, which finally led to an undesired but inevitable divorce, accelerated by the well-meaning but catastrophic interventions (and ethnocentric interpretations) of the wife's parents. I think that we can now easily imagine the overwhelming number of misunderstandings that can spring from conceptions of the couple so different in their presuppositions.

I myself have made my husband (an anthropologist but also an American) "want to disappear under the table" (he says) by bringing up topics at American dinner parties which for me are purely intellectual, like the institution of marriage (a common anthropological subject, nevertheless). I finally got it into my head that if I were critical of the institution, my remarks might be interpreted as a commentary on our own marriage by my American interlocutors. Our American friends have gotten into the habit of considering me as "different" and do not take offense, but if by chance I forget myself (there is a big difference between theory and practice) and begin to make such comments in front of strangers, I quickly make sure that my French accent stands out, or else I explain my work on cultural differences.

One anecdote: in a seminar on cultural analysis, after my presentation of these differences among French and American couples, my American students expressed doubts and said that they found themselves to be quite similar to French couples, and that what I had said might have been true for their parents' generation, but not for them. I suggested a kind of psychodrama and asked the students to form couples and to act as if they were real couples together at a restrauant (a situation they chose as likely). The volunteers began a conversation (in English at my request), spontaneously adopting the discourse and the style of interaction appropriate to the context (young American students among themselves). Someone spoke about the latest film, and the tone quickly became quite natural, with conversation taking place among the couples. Then someone said that he didn't like the film, which provoked a reaction on the part of his partner: "But I always thought you liked that kind of film." And there, to everyone's surprise (including the actors'), the conversation turned away from the group to the couple, who were now facing each other ("I said that to please you, because you hate . . . "). This disagreement, this rupture in the conversation, quickly forced the other couples to intervene ("hey, you guys!"). After a moment of stunned silence, they each commented on the fact that the threat of an argument seemed very real to them, and that it had caused them to become tense. One remark: this little experiment also shows that if American couples avoid contradicting each other in public, it is because the conflict also makes the spectators feel ill at ease, forces them to witness something in "bad taste," and forces them to intervene (that is, to do violence to their feelings and break the taboo against meddling).

When one thinks of all the "scenes" that continually take place between certain French couples ("X had another one of his crises yesterday. He made a huge scene, as usual . . . but everything's all right today"), we can easily imagine the distance separating the French and Americans in this respect. I am not suggesting that happy heterocultural couples do not exist or that they are impossible. But I think that it is very important to realize how differences in our cultural premises can give rise to misunderstandings which we incorrectly attribute to personality differences. In today's world, in which the intercultural couple is becoming common, it is urgent that we understand the precise nature of these relationships.

I would therefore like to go over a few of the cultural premises that can be drawn from the preceding analysis.

On the French side:

1. The stability of the couple is created by the possibility (the freedom) to be myself, to be accepted (and, ideally, desired) as I am, with my faults as well as my strong points ("I can't help it, that's the way I am"). By making my partner the butt of my jokes, for example, I show the solidity, and the special nature of the bonds uniting us.

2. Our affective ties and our conduct are separate; one is not necessarily a reflection of the other. Thus, we can easily accept that a couple may spend their time fighting but that "this doesn't prevent them from loving each other."

3. Affective ties are not necessarily synonymous with harmony. On the contrary, *de la haine à l'amour, il n'y a qu'un pas* (literally, "from hate to love, the distance is only one step"); one is indifferent to one's enemies. Harmony can dangerously resemble indifference, boredom, weariness—that is to say, the death of love, the humdrum, the bland routine, the quiet little life—in short, exactly the opposite of passion, which we associate with a life full of ups and downs, perhaps, but at least with an interesting life ("At least with X, you're never bored").

4. Although they oscillate between the two extremes in which they reproduce relationships of inequality (in which one is paternal or the other is maternal), a couple's relationship is considered to be a relationship of equality or, rather, of equilibrium in its complementarity.

5. Insofar as I can never have a relationship of equality (although I can be friendly) with my parents or my children, the only relationships of equality I can have are with my brothers and sisters (if there isn't too great an age difference) or with my friends. The relationships of the first category (with my siblings) are stamped with sexual taboos, whereas those of the second category (with my friends) represent either an approved type of homophilia (in the case of friends of the same sex) or a refusal to sexuality (in the case of friends of the opposite sex). In this context, the terms "friends" and "lovers" are mutually exclusive (see the chapter on friendship). Ideally, therefore, the couple's relationship reproduces the first type (brother/sister) and the second (friends), with the addition of one distinctive element which characterizes the couple and differentiates it from these two categories: permitted and socially approved sexuality. We (French) do not expect that brothers and sisters, or friends, will never quibble (which does not cast doubt on the affective bonds). On the contrary, by showing that we can allow ourselves such behavior, we are affirming the strength of these affective bonds. The same is true for the (French) couple.

On the American side:

1. The stability of the couple is created by the fact that my partner encourages me to be as I would like to be. Given that I would like to be "perfect," support, sympathy (in the full sense), understanding, and harmony will help me to arrive at my goal. Criticism, reproach, disagreement, and contradiction are therefore, by definition, destructive.

2. Affective bonds and behavior reflect each other. The space I place between my partner and myself, literally and by means of my discourse, is a symptom of disunion.

3. Affective bonds are the equivalent of harmony. All conflict threatens this harmony. Passion can be dangerously reminiscent of the phenomena which destroy harmony (alcohol, drugs, gambling, workaholism, etc.).

4. To love means to trust, and to be able to predict and satisfy all the other's needs. Surprises tend to be feared.

5. To the extent that each person needs the other to satisfy his or

her desires (encouragement, sympathy, support), the couple's relationship can only be a relationship of interdependency, or of alternating dependency.

6. To the extent that the only relationship of dependency that I have known (and accepted) is the relationship with my parents (see the chapter on this relationship), which is stamped with sexual taboos, the relationship I have as part of a couple will, ideally, reproduce this relationship, with the addition of one distinctive element, which characterizes the couple and differentiates it: permitted and socially approved sexuality. I do not expect the ideal parent to criticize me, correct me, or humiliate me but rather to encourage me to surpass myself and support me in my efforts. The same is true of my (American) partner.

# 5   Friendship

When I was in Nukuoro (an atoll in the Pacific where I did fieldwork), a minor incident both surprised and made a great impression on me.

Two or three months after our arrival, nearly all the inhabitants of the village (and hence of the island) went on a picnic together, on another one of the atoll's islets at the other side of the lagoon. After some hesitation. I decided not to join them, fearing that an entire day of tropical picnicking and two crossings of the lagoon in a canoe I found incredibly narrow would not exactly be ideal for my six-month-old daughter. Early in the morning (before it got too hot), the elegant Nukuoro sailing canoes carried people and food to the other side of the lagoon. I was savoring the silence and tranquility of the strangely deserted village. I was finally getting a rest from the native tongue, which had surrounded me ceaselessly, night and day, since our arrival. I remember this sensation very well, this impression of floating in a neutral space, a space that seemed emptied of language, of culture, and of geography.

A loud voice broke the silence. A tall, gaunt, somewhat abrupt woman, my neighbor, had come to bring me a gift of coconut and taro. I invited her in, as was expected. She then announced that she had "come to keep me company so that I wouldn't be alone," as soon as she realized that I had stayed behind in the village. I thanked her, we chatted, and as soon as was politely possible I told her that I appreciated her visit very much but was tired and needed to rest. I had forgotten that she was a well-known specialist in local medicine. She offered to care for me. Secretly blushing at my stubbornness, I once again tried politely to regain the solitude, which was otherwise rarely possible. In vain. She absolutely refused to "abandon me," and declared that from that moment on, we were "friends," that friends gave each other gifts, and that she had brought me the basket of food to seal our "friendship."

It didn't take long for me to learn about friendship. She soon declared something of this nature: "Now that we're friends, I will really teach you to speak Nukuoro correctly, because you speak well, but like a child. You make many mistakes. I know everyone tells you that you speak well, but now I am going to correct you all the time so that you will really speak like us." Having been the first "white" woman and the first "foreigner" to learn the language, I had quickly become a local curiosity, a great source of pride for the people of Nukuoro, whose language, according to the Micronesians of the other islands, was impossible to learn. Her words therefore shook my complacency all the more. She kept her promise, and we eventually became "friends" in a sense closer to my own.

I have never forgotten this scene, and I can still see it in detail. I always considered this moment as very significant, but for reasons that were not always clear to me. Now I think that its importance came from the deep cultural shock I must have experienced at that moment, clouded by other feelings (a kind of guilt for not participating in the picnic, the pleasure of the unexpected solitude, annoyance at seeing it interrupted, annoyance at this annoyance, etc.). What seems particularly important to me is the shock that this incident brought to my concept of friendship. This woman declared herself my friend point blank, without even asking me, in a way that I guessed would be irrevocable. What is more, she seemed to be according me an extraordinary favor. Where I come from, dear lady, I thought to myself, one does not unilaterally declare oneself someone's friend. One "becomes" a friend, and this is based on mutual (though tacit) agreement.

I have told this story only to show how it shed light on my culture, since it provoked a disjunction at a deep level, a disjunction which I do not believe manifested itself in my behavior or in my reaction to the situation. I did what was correct, but I did not "comprehend," in the full sense of the word.

Indeed, in French one "is" a brother, a sister, or parent, one "falls" in love, but one "becomes" a friend. This means that we accept family ties and the affection which in principle goes along with them; we fall in love by accident, almost in spite of ourselves; but we enter voluntarily, by choice, into a friendship. Of course we meet our friends by accident, as we do those with whom we fall in love; our brothers and sisters, on the other hand, are simply there, a part of the family we can reject but with whom we have ties that cannot be annulled or rendered totally nonexistent by a simple act of will. We have always heard that friends are the brothers and sisters we choose, which means that friendship is chosen, kinship is submitted to (often with joy, fortunately, but submitted to nonetheless).

Another relationship which is "imposed from without," but in another manner, is the relationship we have with lovers or sweethearts. We do not resist something that is stronger than ourselves, that is based on sexual attraction. We may choose to marry the person we love (although the "choice" is not always so obvious), but we do not choose those with whom we are in love. Literature has yet to exhaust this subject.

Friendship is therefore the only strong relationship freely chosen and consented to, based neither on family ties nor on sexual attraction. The affection one has for one's friends is similar to that which one has for one's brothers, but the relationship is free of competition (for parental love or that of other family members) and therefore of jealousy and ambiguity. But, like love, friendship carries an element of chance: we are attracted to a person we happen to meet at school, where we live, at a party, and so on. We become closer and closer until a friendship is formed. But we do not declare ourselves someone's "friend," like the woman in Nukuoro did. It is (in French) a relationship based on fact and not on intentions (one does not become someone's friend as one becomes a member of a secret society). Unlike love, however, friendship is characterized by stability and security. I do not have to seduce a friend, in the broadest sense of the word: a friend is a friend to the extent that he or she accepts me as I am; I am not an ink blot for a friend, as I may be for a lover. In principle our relationship is clear, with no gray area or complications, which explains why we are not surprised to hear "We got divorced but we remained very good friends," "Since their divorce, they're the best of friends," and other such variations.

Does this mean that friendship is a "residue of love" (an expression that I have often heard, but always hated)? If we were to consider only the divorce mentioned above, this would seem to be true. Yet, it would undoubtedly be more fruitful to consider another possibility: in the case of a couple who is divorcing (or separating) but who remains

friendship. The heterosexual context is, moreover, the only one in
which two people can "declare themselves friends" with the sole
intention, it seems to me, of eliminating any hint of sexuality from the
relationship. This explains the "let's be friends" common to lovers'
breakups but also the way which I introduce a person to others. If I, a
woman, introduce a man (in French) by saying "This is my friend"
("*C'est mon ami*"), using the possessive, I define the relationship as
sexual. If I want to avoid these connotations, I have to say "this is one
of my friends," "a very dear friend," "a very old friend," "a childhood
friend," "a friend of the family," and so on. The same is true in the
inverse situation.

While I may not declare point-blank "let's be friends," the fact
remains that a tacit pact has been sealed between my friend and me. A
pact, even a tacit one, implies all sorts of contractual agreements and
obligations as well as taboos. It is, of course, in this domain that the
foreigner will run into numerous misunderstandings. In Nukuoro, it
was easy for me to respond to the woman's declaration, "we are
friends," while wondering what I had to do to deserve this friendship.
Her gift of food and the fact that she had come so that "I wouldn't be
alone" already gave me an inkling of the obligations and forms of
demonstration required. It was also apparent that I could not refuse
this friendship without serious consequences. This woman, with her
understanding of intercultural problems, had made things easier for
me. My foreignness, my incontestable difference (physical as well as
linguistic and cultural), had facilitated our becoming close. She had
probably figured that I would never guess it all by myself and that it
was best to explain things to me right away.

Unfortunately, this is not what happens in the majority of cases. I have
often heard French people declare that Americans "have no sense of
friendship," "don't know what friendship is," or else "have only very
superficial relationships." A personal experience may serve as an il-

lustration. One of my friends, a French woman who had been living in the United States for two years but who had been living outside of France for a long time, came to my house one day to unburden herself of the built-up resentment she had been harboring not against me, but against her "neighbor-friends." I hadn't seen her for a few days, as is frequent in large cities, and had called her to "check things out." Over the phone, she told me that she had been "very tired," that the kids were wearing her out, and that she had been "beat" for the past two days. I immediately offered to take care of her children so that she could rest, and she accepted right away. Fifteen or twenty minutes later, she arrived at my house to drop off the kids and, presumably, to go back to rest all afternoon. But instead of leaving right away to take full advantage of the free time available to her, she stayed nearly two hours at my house. Without realizing it, I had triggered something with the offer, which to me had seemed only natural. While at my house, she complained bitterly about the fact that her neighbor, an American woman whom she considered to be a good friend, had not made the same offer: "Do you think she said 'I'll take care of the children so you can rest?' Do you think she brought me a dish so that I wouldn't have to cook? No, nothing. She only asks me 'how I'm doing,' every day. . . . What a hypocrite." A flood of similar reproaches followed. Then came some nostalgia for France, where people know what friendship is. Then a grateful smile: "Luckily you're here, because you know what friendship is; you see, you immediately offered to take the kids. . . . Whereas Americans, they would just let you croak."

People say that a friend is someone in whom you can confide, whom you can "ask to do anything," on whom you can call in case of an emergency. Why didn't my friend ask her neighbor friend to "take the children off her hands?" Did she ask me to do it, in fact? No, I offered; she accepted. It seemed natural to me, as it did to her.

There is, in fact, a gap between what we say we can do (ask something of a friend) and what we expect (which is that the friend will "spontaneously" offer to do what we would otherwise have had to ask of him or her). But since the friend must be informed, we start off by telling him that we have a "problem," and we disclose the situation. If the friend is a "real friend," he or she should intervene, take charge of the situation, so to speak, and propose a solution, namely, his or her help. This calls for the response: "Oh, no, I don't want to bother you," "You're sure you wouldn't mind?" and other phrases which express my concern for the friend's well-being. And it is then the friend's turn to insist: "Of course not, I don't mind at all. What are friends for if you can't count on them to help you with silly things like this?" And the friend in need, who didn't have to ask for anything, can then give in: "If you insist . . ."

Of course this exchange is only a model and can happen in several different ways, but this is roughly what is expected of a friend. This explains why we (French) are not surprised to see a friend take control of a situation and to announce in a peremptory manner, "Nothing doing. I'll pick you up at eight and we'll go to the movies. You're beat, you need to relax, I'm not going to stay here doing nothing while you work yourself to death right before my eyes"; or, "Don't make a fuss; we're taking you with us to the country this weekend. It will do you loads of good, and you can't say no."

An American would undoubtedly shy away from such authority. It would represent an unbearable invasion of the other person's private life and, what is worse, would suggest that he or she is incapable of managing his or her own affairs, of getting on alone. We can now understand why my French friend's American neighbor would have hesitated to "bring her a dish so that she wouldn't have to cook" or to offer to take care of the children. This would have meant that the neighbor had noticed my friend was incapable of taking care of her children and that the children were suffering as a result of it, or that they were behaving like "abandoned children." Offering to intervene would have meant passing moral judgment and would have been a condemnation of my friend, who, far from appreciating the gesture, would have taken it as a slap in the face had she been American.

An American colleague confirmed my interpretation, without even being aware of it at first. It was the end of an especially difficult university semester—a time associated always with overwork and fatigue—and we were consoling each other with mutual complaints and jokes. Concerning work, I brought up the name of a mutual (American) colleague in whose research I was interested. At the mention of this woman's name, my colleague's face lit up with an understanding smile, which was explained by the following confidential remark: "I like L. very much, and we're good friends, but she has one fault that drives me crazy. Yesterday, for example, I was heading for a meeting and I ran into her. . . . She offered to take care of Jackie at her house whenever I want, so that I can catch my breath a bit . . . as if I were incapable of taking care of my daughter and my work at the same time. That bugs me." I couldn't resist, and I told her about the cultural misunderstanding between my friend and her neighbor (discussed above); she laughed and confirmed my interpretation. Yes, she had felt invaded and insulted by the offer which this woman, whom she liked very much, had made to her and which she had quickly refused. Thinking about this case later on, I wondered how it was possible for an American to commit such a blunder. Upon inquiring, I discovered, to my great relief, that in fact the woman in question came from a bicultural family.

Friendship is considered, both by Americans and by the French, to be a special relationship. However, this universe of "perfect understanding" becomes literally a mine field in intercultural relationships because it is in those areas that I consider to be most profoundly "natural" that I can wound without knowing it. Indeed, how can I imagine that the "best" of me, this "generosity" toward the other, can be taken as a quasi-hostile act on my part?

What is particularly disturbing here is that, from a purely descriptive viewpoint, the American and French conceptions of friendship seem to be identical. At first glance, it might seem that the French have more nuances at their disposal to specify the exact nature of the relationship, because the word "friend" is used much more loosely in American than the word *ami* is in French. Since an American will use the term "a friend" when speaking of someone he or she hardly knows, it is tempting for a French person to conclude that he or she is promiscuous. For an American, however, this is merely a verbal shortcut which saves the trouble of explaining the differences between "friend" and all the other terms available (acquaintance, vague acquaintance, buddy, pal, chum, roommate, housemate, classmate, schoolmate, teammate, playmate, companion, co-worker, colleague, childhood friend, new friend, old friend, very old friend, family friend, close friend, very close friend, best friend, girlfriend, boyfriend, etc.).

Beyond this misleading superficial difference, the concept of friendship, as it is defined on both sides of the Atlantic, includes strangely similar, if not identical, categories. A friend is someone I love like a brother or sister, someone I trust, someone whose company I enjoy, someone on whom I can depend, someone who understands me, and someone with whom I can be myself, let the mask drop, someone who doesn't judge me, someone who doesn't try to change me, who knows and accepts me as I am, in whom I can safely confide, and for whom I am all of the above. But as the previously mentioned case shows, it is not the category that proves to be the source of cultural misunderstanding but rather the presuppositions that enter into this category, which can be very different. Thus, in the case of my friend and her neighbor, the axiom "friends help each other" is valid both for Americans and for the French. Yet according to my interpretation, the misunderstanding arises from different presuppositions, which are roughly these: "X is my friend, he is therefore going to offer to help me" (French side); "X is my friend, he will therefore ask me to help him if he needs me" (American side).

If I want to understand the intercultural difficulties possible in this domain, I must therefore question not the categories but what they entail that is unsaid, their implicit "truths."

It would take too long to mention the many cases that aroused my curiosity, or the interviews that enabled me to arrive at my interpretation. I will give only the results of this analysis here, that is to say, my interpretation. I repeat that my goal is not to prove that I am right but to suggest another way of seeing things, to point out an alternate route, the main advantage of which would be to diminish intercultural wounds (the intellectual pleasure is an added bonus). I will simply review the most common characteristics of friendship, those that are constantly mentioned by informants, that appear in newspaper and magazine articles on the subject and in language generally. Of course, I will place the accent on the difference because resemblances, causing no difficulties, do not concern me here.

A friend is someone who understands me "better than anyone else in the world." Americans and French both agree. But what does this word "understand" mean?

John and I are friends, and we are both American. We understand each other, which means that we agree with each other, or in any case we are "supportive" of each other. John must not take my adversary's side; on the contrary, he must agree with me, since he is supposed to be another me. He understands me because he can put himself in my place, and vice versa.

If he confides in me that he did something silly, that he acted very stupidly, my role is not to tell him, "boy, you sure did," but to make him feel better by finding extenuating circumstances, by reminding him of all his good points, and by helping him to have confidence in himself again—I must "give him support and sympathy," "boost his sagging ego," "cheer him up".

Justine and Séraphine, two French women, are friends. When Séraphine has done something stupid and docs not know what to do to make up for it, she turns to Justine, who admits, "You sure were pretty heavy-handed about it." She then helps Séraphine to see clearly and to find a means to patch things up. If this happens repeatedly, Séraphine might begin her story with "You're going to be mad at me again," or else, the problem at hand having finally been resolved, Séraphine, as she is walking out the door, might say to Justine, "Thank you, I feel much better. I knew it was time for me to let you set me straight." This means that my friend understands me because he or she is another me, but in the sense that he or she is the half of me that remains reasonable. My friend is there to tell me out loud what I tell myself confusedly; he or she "shakes me up" (*me secoue les puces*) out of affection for me, without, in doing so, judging me.

If John and Justine become heterocultural friends, it is possible that John will look to Justine for "support" and will be "set straight," in which case he will feel betrayed; it is possible that Justine will look to John to help her to "see clearly" and will be at a complete loss when he defends her position. This is how a French informant summarized the difficulty she had when speaking of her marital problems to her American friends: "As soon as I began to complain about my husband, they began criticizing Hugh, and I found myself defending him. It was ridiculous."

As we can see, on both sides we agree on one thing: a friend is one of the rare people who understand me. But what my friend will do to show me how much he or she "understands" me will be extremely different depending on whether this friend is French or American.

One of the reasons I have friends, whether I am French or American, is that their presence is pleasurable for me. For French people, this translates into frequent outings together, to restaurants, the movies, picnics, and other activities which vary according to one's age. It is therefore possible for Zoë to invite her friend Géraldine (and Géraldine's partner or husband as the case may be) to dinner at her house several times in a row without Géraldine, who rarely entertains, feeling the least bit bothered. The rule of reciprocity among friends will nonetheless be respected: Géraldine will arrange to give her friend small gifts "for no reason," on no special occasion, will do her favors, will pay for Zoë at the theater or cinema, will take care of her children, or the equivalent. Sometimes, Géraldine's mere presence at one of Zoë's dinners may be a favor to Zoë: the dinner is what we call "a function," and Zoë has asked Géraldine "not to leave her alone."

It seems to me that in a similar situation Americans would prefer exchanges of the same nature. A dinner is held at one person's house and then at the next, although one need not necessarily alternate so strictly. Gifts call for gifts, and so on. This eliminates the possibility that any one person will feel exploited, which would undermine the friendship. Besides, demanding one's "turn" is a means of reinforcing a friendship. In cases where an exchange is practically impossible (a canoe expedition for example), responsibilities will be clearly divided in advance, here again to avoid any dangerous pressure on the bonds of friendship. (This is not to say that there are no Americans who act differently but still manage to keep their friends forever.)

This difference may result from the fact that once a friendship has been established among French people (and we know that this does not happen easily; we've all read *The Little Prince*), it is solid enough to weather all sorts of storms. My friends are familiar with my rotten nature, my obsessions, my mood swings, my habit of putting my foot in my mouth, my tactlessness, whatever. If they are my friends, it is because they know all that about me yet find something that compensates for it and helps them to tolerate my faults, or else because they see themselves in me. The threats to friendship come from elsewhere—a matter I will come back to later.

For Americans, however, even the most solid friendship seems to contain a constant element of fragility. Many dangers threaten it: separation, distance, silence (absence of regular communication, letters, telephone calls, visits), but also all that we could summarize by the words "too much," that is to say, anything that threatens the balance in the relationship, which is based on equality and exchange, on taking turns. Thus, according to one female American informant, a dependency which becomes too strong could signal the end of a relationship. This is how an American male explained the problem posed by disequilibrium: "Timothy and I are in the process of becoming good friends; I can speak freely with him, and vice versa. But I'm getting worried because he seems to consider me his best friend. I like him very much but he will probably never be my best friend because, quite frankly, he's a bit boring. But if he treats me like his best friend, I'm obliged to act as if he were, so as not to hurt him, and he will become a burden, an obligation, a responsibility, which I absolutely do not want."

This insistence on equality and mutuality, which is different from reciprocity, does not strike me as one of the major characteristics of French friendship, which appears to thrive on complementarity, a kind of distribution of tasks.

Thus, as an American, I expect my friend to "drop everything" and rush to help me when I need it. But here again, I must be careful not to cross the "too much" line, not to go beyond the limit. I therefore have the comfort of knowing that my friend "would do anything for me," but I must be sensible enough not to test this conviction beyond what is possible, not to "go too far," for fear of destroying the equilibrium that protects our relationship. This would not be the case in France, where I can share "crisis" after "crisis" with no more remorse than that indicated by a remark such as "I keep bugging you with my problems . . ." The role played by friends was long responsible for the negative image, in France, of having recourse to psychoanalysis (a "sad necessity" for "those who have no friends," "those who have to pay someone to listen to them," etc.). It is also from this perspective that we can understand the success of psychoanalysis in the United States: one refuses to overburden friends with an unfair or uneven sharing of one's problems.

An important characteristic of friendship, on both sides of the Atlantic, is the sharing of secrets. I can tell my friend things I cannot tell my parents, my lover, my children, to mention only those closest to me. I can tell my friends secrets about my parents, my lover, my children. We can speak to each other "with open hearts." According to my information, many French and Americans do just that, or at least have the impression of doing so. On the American side, it is even a kind of obligation, a necessary proof of friendship, maybe the most important one among young people. The "sharing" of these revelations about one's "self," one's infatuations, and one's sex life, is almost a ritual among young people. If I do not "share," my friend will suspect me of not "giving," and this will wind up destroying our friendship. One also tells "secrets" to friends ("He tells me things he tells nobody else"; "She tells me things that no one else knows about"). I will therefore consider myself to be the exclusive repository of my friends' secrets, tacitly sworn to complete discretion. This situation has interesting implications. The first is that I must have enough secrets to be able to share one with each of my friends. (If I have fewer secrets, does that mean I will have fewer friends?) The second implication is that I will feel betrayed if I learn that I am not the sole repository of a particular secret; hence the feeling of possessive jealousy which logically has no place in friendship. The third implication is that, in order to be assured of total secrecy, I will keep my friends from becoming friends, or even keep them from meeting each other. This would imply that American friendships are generally dyadic in nature. And they are, in fact, in a manner worth examining.

In my observations of American children, some of their phrases surprised me (as a foreigner) and caught my attention. As we know (see the chapter on parents and children), American parents encourage their children to "make friends" very early on. These are two sentences that the children learn very quickly, as early as four or five years old, and which they repeat often: "Jill (John) is my best friend"; and "You are not my friend any more," or "I am not your friend any more." The second sentence comes up as soon as one child is contradicted by the other, or it is used to ward off such a contradiction. What it means, essentially, is "if you do not agree with me, you cannot be my friend." It comes up just as frequently when a child feels cheated because a friend did not allow him or her to "have his (or her) turn" (and, for example, have the chance to play different roles). The child will complain that the friend "never lets me have a turn." This suggests that being a friend means above all not arguing, with all the demands this implies. As a result, for an American, the word "friend" is a title one must constantly merit, of which one must constantly prove oneself worthy, and which therefore demands vigilance and effort.

As it is difficult always to agree with several people at one time, children will have a tendency to be "friends" in twos, even if these dyads are not always the same: today Bob plays with Rob (classmate), tomorrow with Zig (whom he met at his swimming lessons), and the day after tomorrow with Mortimer (his neighbor), and so on. It is very likely that Rob, Zig, and Mortimer never play together and that they have never met. Bob is loyal to each one in turn. It is even possible that Bob will play only one hour with Zig, because Mortimer is coming to play with him after that. And it will not occur to Zig to stay after Mortimer arrives, because he has learned that he would probably not be included in the games. I have often had occasion to see an American child tell his mother he is going to his neighbor's house to play, only to see him return shortly afterward, sulking, and report that "X was there, and they were playing together," or, if the situation is really serious, "they wouldn't let me play with them." When speaking of Rob, Zig, or Mortimer, Bob may say "He is my best friend," without seeing any contradiction therein.

While these distinctions become more refined and nuanced with adulthood, they still remain paradigmatic. As an American, I will construct my friendships along two intersecting planes. The first is horizontal and in the shape of a starfish with myself in the middle. Each branch constitutes one of my friendships. The second plane is vertical and rises in the form of a pyramid, reflecting the hierarchy of my friendships. For my friends at the top of the pyramid, I will reserve all my care, my constant vigilance, my greatest efforts, my atten- tiveness, and my time—in short, the best of me. Clearly, there can be but a privileged few at this level (according to an American dictum, "He who can count his friends on all the fingers of one hand is lucky") and only one at the summit.

This does not mean that I cannot appreciate, to varying degrees, the company of the many people with whom I get along well. The strength of my friendships with these people will be inversely propor- tional to the place on my pyramid. The base of this pyramid, where the greatest number of people are, therefore corresponds to my most tenuous bonds, those people whose company I enjoy from time to time—to dine with, for example, or at parties. It is precisely to these American social exchanges that the French have easiest access, for even if they are not fully integrated in this complex system—perhaps just "passing through"—they themselves will be part of the base of this pyramid, where there is constant movement. It is therefore not sur- prising that these same French people judge Americans to be "superficial," "incapable of true friendship," and so on, since they will probably never have the opportunity to experience American friendship (the summit of the pyramid) in action. What they do see in abundance, on the other hand, is American "sociability," which values "popularity," one's aptitude for "making new friends." These relationships are not superficial as the French understand them ("incapable of depth") but are intentially superficial in the American sense: they must remain on the surface because that is where the nature of pleasure lies; the pleasure of the moment with neither attachments nor obligations; the pleasure of chance encounters; the pleasure of seduction; the pleasure of small talk; the pleasure of an "agreeable evening," whatever one's conception of this may be (an elegant dinner, or a bash with drugs, alcohol, sex, dancing, intellectualism, or whatever), much like the thrill of exploring a foreign neighborhood or making a foray into an exotic restaurant.

For a French person, difficulty often arises because, due to the small number of guests present at a dinner, he or she mistakes a "social" gathering for an intimate one. The American who invited him or her probably didn't help the matter by announcing that there would be "just a few friends." This difference, which is more than just linguistic, is all the more disturbing for French people who, traditionally, do not invite "just anyone" to dinner. I know that customs are changing, especially in Paris where people reproachfully say that everything is becoming "Americanized"; the fact remains that it is easy, if only by looking at the way the table is set and thus deducing what menu is planned, to know what sort of dinner one is attending. (One need not be French for this. Many Americans have quickly learned to recognize the signs.) If these indications are not enough, one has only to open one's ears and listen or to observe the nonverbal exchanges among the guests (clothing, facial expressions, the way people carry themselves). In ten minutes, the difference is established between a dinner with friends and a dinner with colleagues (which might occur only once a year). But these signs are not immediately apparent at an American dinner, hence the confusion.

While a French person may find Americans to be "superficial in their friendships" for the above-mentioned reasons and may accuse them of promiscuity, an American may come to consider French friendships rather stifling. In the beginning, when he is first invited and feels "admitted into the intimacy" of the French, he is happy, he sings the praises of French friendship, repeats what French people say about Americans. Yes, it is true, he affirms, Americans are superficial in their friendships, not like the French. He quickly gets to know the circle (the choice of this word is intentional) of friends of his new friend, since there cannot be any get-together of even slight importance without them, and he sees them often since they also begin inviting him regularly, begin including him in their little group's activities. And then one day, a heightened sense of claustrophobia seizes him and he's "had enough." Enough of seeing the same faces daily, enough of the discussions bordering on dispute, enough of not being able to say no without seeming like a party pooper, enough of being ceaselessly teased, enough of feeling invaded, enough of the telephone calls that take so much time "for nothing," enough of the unexpected interruptions, enough of the constant changes in definite plans—in short, he's had enough of playing at being French. He feels as if he is in an aquarium and needs air, wants to head out to sea.

And yet this foreigner's interpretation should not be a surprise. Indeed, what this fictive (?) American is reacting against is the closure of the circle of friends which evokes, and in a sense reproduces, the closure of the family circle. According to the French conception, friendships are parallel to family relationships, except that they are bonds we choose and for which we assume full responsibility, perhaps even assuring these bonds priority over kinship ties. They can even serve as substitutes: I can create a "family" of my choosing with my friends. (These bonds sometimes are spoken of ironically, as in the expression "you're a mother to me".) From this perspective, it is logical for me to introduce my friends to each other in the hope that they will get along ("You'll see, she's very nice"). If I like them and each of them likes me, they cannot help but like each other. If it were otherwise, this would signal an error in judgment on my part. Furthermore, I often speak of my friends to my other friends, so they already know each other before they meet. I am, in addition, somewhat obliged to introduce them if I do not want to be teased with comments like "Well, how much longer are you going to hide this marvelous creature from us?"; "Tell me, you're sure you didn't make up this friend?"; "Are you ashamed of her?"; and so on.

As time goes by, these bonds consolidate and become firm until they reach the point where they lose all contingency. At this point they become nearly indestructible, and there is total trust. A rupture can be caused only by a betrayal, and this is accompanied by a very deep—maybe even traumatizing—emotional shock. What I cannot understand is how I, who thought I knew someone so well (since we were friends), could have "been so wrong" about him or her.

According to the American conception, my friendship is, in a sense, a precious object, a "treasure," which I deposit with a chosen few. A treasure shared by thousands is no longer a treasure. Similarly, my love is not inexhaustible, cannot reach many without weakening and risking depletion. I will therefore seek those who will be worthy of my treasure, and I will withdraw it if they cease to be so. However strong the friendship may be, it always retains an element of contingency, a threat of rupture. If I discover that my friend is no longer deserving of my treasure, for reasons which I need justify to no one, I take it away and look to place it elsewhere. Disappointed, I will say, "I misplaced my trust."

This quest for the ideal friend in some ways reproduces the quest for love. As an American, in friendship as in love (see the chapter on the couple), I will search for someone who supports me, approves of me, gives back to me a confirmation of myself, loves in me the person I want to be, and helps me to become that person. I must devote myself to keeping up these ties of friendship, to maintaining them, to being worthy of them, or else I risk being a "bad friend" ("I've been a bad friend this month"), which with time could mean losing my friends. But it is more in my friendships (which are, in principle, devoid of sexuality) than in my couple relationship that I will find equality, mutual trust, understanding, and a person in whom I can confide. Ideally, my lover or my spouse will also be my best friend. The dream of the perfect dyad is common to many Americans. Thus, it is not unusual to see John and Mary's relationship as a couple become their only significant affective relationship, to the exclusion of family and friends. According to an American informant, "I realized after my divorce that I didn't have a single friend: I had lost contact with my friends after my marriage, and for years I was happy to devote all my time to my family (maybe more to my children than to my wife, in fact) and to my work."

The eminently social nature of friendship is apparent in the negative attitudes of both Americans and the French concerning those who "have no friends." A person who has no friends in disquieting because he has no attachments (and I therefore have no hold over him). It seems to me, nonetheless, that even in this context there is a slight difference in meaning.

I believe that such a person, if French, would inspire a certain pity; even the most "horrible" people—criminals, assassins, and the like— can have friends. The fact that this character has no friends means that no one has ever found anything in him or her to love, that he or she is incapable of loving and of being loved, a fate more sad then frighten- ing. But for an American, the "loner," that solitary person one reads about in the paper, is a disturbing anomaly. This is because the presupposition, it seems to me, is that anyone can be loved if he or she makes an effort; therefore if a person is alone, it can only be by choice.

In other words, a French person without friends would be asocial, whereas an American "loner" would be antisocial.

# 6 The Telephone

It may seem strange for the telephone to be given the same attention as friendship or the family. Yet the telephone is part of our daily lives and therefore of our relational space. Impressive technological developments transform it every day. But only the gadget itself changes, not our way of communicating, which obeys the same implicit rules, whether we use an old-fashioned phone or sophisticated "tele-cards" and computers. And we now know that whenever we say "implicit" we will find possible cultural misunderstandings.

A French woman with impeccable English who had been living in the United States for three or four years and who was about to return to France told me, "Sometimes I still get irritated because there are many things which I really don't understand. . . . I have an American friend . . . we really get along very, very well . . . and I know she has some very big family problems. Last Christmas, she went home, and I knew that she and her mother would be going at it. I called her Christmas evening. . . . She told me that she couldn't stay on the phone, that she would call me back to explain. Christmas came and went. Nothing. Okay, I tell myself that she must have had even more problems that she expected. I called her on New Year's Day to wish her a happy new year, and the same thing happened; she told me to call her back, which I absolutely refused to do. I said no and hung up. She didn't even inquire about Patrick, who, as she knew very well, had come back from India to spend the holidays with me. Patrick was quite surprised. . . . In the end she called back. I thought about the cultural differences you and I talked about, and instead of keeping my mouth shut, instead of swallowing my anger and burning up about it by myself, I decided to tell her that in my culture, it was impolite to act as she had acted. I'm glad I did, because we talked it over and cleared it up. . . . She had, in fact, had many problems."

An American, speaking about the French friends she has in France, said, "They hate using the telephone. Here, if you're moving around a lot and have no time to write, you use the phone. Whereas if they have no time to write, they don't call either, nothing, just silence."

As a French academic in the United States, for a long time I was flabbergasted by the apparent ease with which students called my house to ask what I judged to be "trivial" questions, questions which, I thought, certainly could have waited until I was in my office.

The telephone plays a very complicated role in the lives of French people. If we can afford it, we have a telephone installed as quickly as possible. But once installed, we subject it to all sorts of unspoken rules, as if it represented a threat that we had allowed into our homes, a kind of Trojan horse whose presence we know to be necessary ("if something were to happen . . .") but whose power must be contained, limited. For some people, it even seems that the ideal telephone would be a transmitter, allowing you to make calls, but without a receiver, which "rings" you as it pleases.

Nevertheless, the telephone is a common item today, whose use is familiar to everyone. Why then does it retain this ambiguous nature?

To know whom I can call and when, I need more than a guide to etiquette. Indeed, for a French person, using the telephone affirms the nature of a relationship. But, as you may have guessed, this is not the case for an American.

I (a French person) call an office to ask for information. The phone is answered politely but rapidly, giving me the impression that if I do not hurry to ask all my questions, the party at the other end will hang up. I therefore have the impression of retaining that party against his or her will, and if I press him or her, I will be made to feel that I am going too far ("if everyone were like you . . ."). Perhaps the feeling here is that by telephoning, I am somehow cheating, since I am not waiting in line, I am not waiting my turn like everyone else. (Is this why waiting has been reinstituted for the telephone, with music following the unavoidable *"ne quittez pas"* — "please hold"?) There may also be another explanation: behind the counter, the employee holds a certain power over the client which he or she loses at the end of the line. In order to reestablish the norm, the employee "gets rid of me" by forcing me to hurry, or demotes me to the position of the one-who-asks by making me wait.

If I call someone who occupies a position of the slightest importance, I must immediately identify myself by answering the insistent question *"de la part de qui?"* ("who's calling?"). Suddenly, I am transformed into a potential nuisance. (The American response, "may I ask who is calling," which is closer in meaning to *"qui dois-je annoncer,"* is less and less frequent, replaced by the master phrase "He (she) is in conference right now; may I have him (her) call you back," which allows one to avoid nuisances.)

In the case, then, of a business transaction (calling an office, an agency, or a public service), the call may be unpleasant, but it is clear-cut. In calling, I put myself at the mercy of the person answering the phone. If I am still not satisfied, my only alternative is to hang up, which does not resolve the question about which I called and is therefore not in my best interest. I believe this explains, in part, why many French people prefer to go to the agency or office in question in order to obtain information that an American would get by telephone. When I am there in person, I cannot be made to disappear so easily, and if I am in the least bit motivated (or stubborn) I will spend "as much time as is necessary," but I will leave satisfied.

Further, the person who answers the telephone cannot be confronted in case of an error or mistaken information but remains "a lady," "a man," "they." If I ask to whom I am speaking, the person will give me his or her first name, in a country where I do not often allow just anyone to call me by my first name. But then, it is not really the first name, but rather "Tell them Monsieur André," or "Ask for Madame Anna." All this suggests a certain degree of wariness with respect to official transactions performed over the telephone. One feels, in a sense, alone against an indistinct body of evasive responders. Several French people have admitted to not having confidence in information obtained by telephone because they had learned from experience that "a response over the phone commits no one." Thus: "I called the store twice, I asked if they had an accessory for my camera, I gave the brand name and the number, and I was told they had it. I was a bit wary, so I called back the next day, and said outright, 'You have it? Are you sure? I can come pick it up right away?' 'Yes, yes, yes.' I went there and they didn't have it. I told them that I had called, etc. 'It was a mistake' was all they said."

The desire to know with whom one is dealing is expressed in another context by the incongruous *"qui est là?"* or *"qui est à l'appareil?"* ("who is this?") which often assails me when I answer the phone. It is as if someone were to knock at your door and ask you to identify yourself. In order to make sense of this sort of question, which seems ridiculous or aberrant, I think we must consider it in another light. By asking the person who answers the telephone "who is this?" I am affirming a close relationship between the responder and myself. What my question really means is "which one of you has answered the telephone"—that is to say, "which of the regulars of the house," implying by "regulars" those "whom I know and who are in a position to answer the phone" (members of the family, housekeeper, baby-sitters, in-laws, intimate friends). In this case, answering with just a first name will suffice.

For similar reasons (to affirm a close relationship), French people do not identify themselves on the telephone, as opposed to Americans, who often give their full names even if they know the person fairly well. When a French person gives his or her name, it is proof of a distant, "formal" relationship, since all those who consider themselves to be "good friends" will not give their names when they call. It is up to you to recognize the sound of a friend's voice and to do so without hesitating. We expect to be recognized, even if we do not call frequently, and even if we know that the person called knows "loads of people." It even becomes a game, a kind of coquetry, a test of friendship to which we subject the uncertain responder. For fear of making a mistake, therefore, we quickly learn to recognize people by their voices, which in turn reinforces the system. Distance in time and space does not diminish this expectation. I myself have received telephone calls literally from the four corners of the earth and from people I had not seen "for ages." This did not prevent them from not giving their names; quite the contrary. And of course, I always eventually recognized them, even if I had to pretend to during the first thirty seconds of conversation.

What happens in the most common case, that of telephone calls between people who know each other and see one another frequently?

Here again, the ease with which one picks up the telephone to call someone indicates the nature of the relationship between the caller and the person called. The telephone call should in fact be seen as an unannounced visit. It is as though I were ringing someone's bell without having given warning that I was coming. Of course there is always the possibility of not answering, of letting the caller ring. In the case of a door, I can use the peep hole if I want to know who is ringing. But if I want to know who is calling, I must pick up the phone (unless I have an answering machine which allows this sort of spying). The call is thus a disruption of my home, of my life. As for the unexpected visit, I can resort to all sorts of escape mechanisms if I want to avoid it ("I was just going out"), but in the case of the phone I have less control over the exchange with the other person: I cannot see his or her face (is this person disappointed? angry? ruffled? indifferent?). Furthermore, I am cut off from all sorts of signs on which I normally depend in my interpersonal exchanges: a facial expression, a look in the eyes, a smile, a grimace, a movement, gestures, the possible presence of other people whom I cannot see, the overall setting, and so on. Hence there is a certain uneasiness.

A telephone call often implies the making of a rapid decision, the setting of a time and a place for an appointment, for example, followed by a temporary loss of contact (which prevents any changes). This, for many French people, represents a somewhat unpleasant pressure. We like to put off the moment when we must commit ourselves, we like to keep a certain flexibility so as not to find ourselves "trapped" by several engagements due to our own miscalculation. Thus, when we are friends in high school (*lycée*), for example, we "stop by" each other's houses, we "pick each other up." But when we are older, and very busy, we part knowing that we'll see each other soon (tomorrow?), but to set the details, we plan to call each other— *"on s'appelle."*

This *on s'appelle* which ends many conversations is not the last chance one has to put off (or simply to avoid) a decision. Once on the telephone, there is still *"je te rappelle"* ("I'll call you back") which can play the same role.

We might think that the telephone could be used to announce an upcoming visit ("I was in the neighborhood . . ."). But this is not the case. If we are forewarned of an imminent visit, we feel compelled to be more or less ready to receive it. Hence the potential for panic (we quickly send one of the kids to pick up some pastries or something to drink), because we no longer have the excuse of not being in a position to honor the unexpected guest ("I'm sorry, you've come in the middle of . . . ; There isn't a drop of anything in the house") and of being able to offer just a "cup of coffee."

Although it constitutes a disruption, the telephone call does not carry the same restrictions as the unannounced visit. Subjected to fairly strict rules of etiquette (not early in the morning, not late in the evening, not after 8 p.m., not during lunch, not during nap time, not during dinner), it is still more flexible than the unannounced visit. Disruptions by telephone calls can therefore be more frequent than those by unannounced visits, which explains why we take all sorts of precautions when we call a colleague at home, saying, for example, "I'm sorry to bother you," "Excuse me for calling you at home,' or other similar formulas which are always followed by a "but" which justifies the call. The energy of the "not at all, not at all" in response must either reassure you or indicate that you are indeed calling at a bad time, which is sometimes reinforced by "well I was just. . .".

Is this to say that French people have an unhealthy aversion to the telephone, a paranoid attitude? Certain Americans are not far from thinking so. But the frequent apprehension which accompanies the making of a phone call must be interpreted otherwise. As a matter of fact, this apprehension disappears when it is a question of calling close friends or members of the family with whom one gets along well. In these cases, we know exactly with whom we are dealing, we are familiar with that person's expressions and the inflections of his or her voice, we know when it is best not to call ("never before noon"), at which unusual moments it is acceptable to call ("she is always up until two or three in the morning"), and so on. If I accidentally call at a bad time, the person will tell me so without my getting angry.

In such cases, the telephone becomes a precious tool. It allows me to bridge the gap caused by spatial or temporal distances, permits the frequent visits that I would like to make or receive but which are impossible due to my schedule and those of my close friends and family, or, perhaps, to the distances which separate us, even within the same city. It is a way of staying in touch with another person, of always being up on his or her state of mind. If I haven't heard from a friend in several days and suspect that "something must be going on", I might, because of the silence and thus the need for action it implies, call or pay a visit "just to know for sure." In these cases of telephone calls among close friends, the nature of the exchange closely resembles the nature of the relationship. We act as we would if we were face to face, we can even reach a greater level of intimacy, but we remain ourselves. The telephone allows us to multiply the exchanges, to instantaneously share a thought, an opinion, a bit of news, a prognosis, one's joy or solitude, a "crisis" or a moment of depression, a "nice surprise," and so on.

The only other case in which I could allow myself to be so impulsive seems to be quite different: if I am very angry with people I don't know because they represent a certain company or supplier (people working in a "customer service" office, for example), I will not hesitate to pick up the telephone to "tell them what I think of them," or to warn them that they're "going to hear from me." In both cases (the telephone call between close friends and family, and the one between strangers), one can be impulsive because the situation is unambiguous. The relationship between the people on either end of the line is clear: in the first case, it is strong (and can therefore allow for this type of disruption) while in the second it is nonexistent or threatens to become so.

In close relationships, telephone calls can take place parallel to visits (it is possible to call as soon as you get home because you had forgotten to say something or because you thought of something new), can supplement visits (fill the gap between visits), or can almost completely replace visits. We call in order to prolong a moment spent with someone, or to reaffirm or reinforce a bond, a contact, and "spend some time" with someone. Specific information is rarely exchanged in this context. It is not a matter of "talking about" something, but very simply of "talking." This does not mean that nothing is learned during these conversations; We may even receive specific answers to our questions. But what is most important is all that is said in the context of this exchange of information, the conversation surrounding it (which sometimes might make us forget the information in question), and, in the case of great distances, the sound of the person's voice, the brief illusion of presence, of proximity.

Thus, in the case of great distances or of infrequent phone calls, we have no qualms about spending large sums of money in order to say little more than "hello, how are you" to all those present at the moment of the call, who get on the phone, one by one, only to say essentially the same thing. In such cases, emotions which are heightened by distance take precedence over everything else, but not to the point of making us forget the ritual requiring that we "say a few words to each person." Moreover, the telephone call can become an outright ritual on important dates: birthdays, holidays, Christmas, or

New Year's. Here again, it is the act of calling that counts, not so much the words (often ritual) that are exchanged. No matter what obligations I may have at the moment of the call, I must also participate in the ritual if I have taken the trouble to answer the phone. If I cannot participate, I will not answer: picking up the telephone to tell a friend ready for ritual that one is not free to participate constitutes an incongruity for a French person. An American in such a situation would tend to prefer even a brief response ("I can't talk now"); the fact that one can allow oneself to give such a response is a sign of a strong relationship. We can now understand the misunderstanding recounted by the French woman at the beginning of this chapter.

The preceding seems to indicate that the telephone has two personalities for the French, depending on the nature of one's relationship with the person called. When the relationship is characterized by certitudes (family, friends), the telephone wire becomes a symbolic extension of the ties linking the caller and the person called. In this case the telephone is reassuring, its presence desirable. In all other cases it represents uncertainty, and therefore anxiety, a threat, an intrusion, an upheaval, a risk of invasion, and uneasiness before the unknown. Further, the way I conduct my telephone exchanges will reproduce the way I conduct my other daily exchanges, for example, my conversations (see the chapter on conversation).

The dividing line is not as clear for Americans and is hence more difficult for foreigners to discover. As an American, I consider the telephone first and foremost as a tool, a practical and indispensable instrument. Even before moving, for example, I arrange to have the telephone installed at my new address, so that it functions from the day I move into my new residence; if I am remaining in the same city, I can usually keep the same number, unless I want to conceal my tracks a little by changing numbers.

My telephone number quickly becomes an integral part of my identity. When I give my name and address, the number follows automatically. It is printed on my checks, accompanies all my credit purchases, and is available to whoever wants to take a poll, perform a market survey, or conduct phone sales. Thanks to this number, I am accessible to an incalculable number of people who might need or desire to reach me, including a great many total strangers. It appears on all sorts of lists, which, until the day I am contacted, I am not even aware exist. Thus it will come as no great surprise if I receive a telephone call from the university I attended thirty or forty years ago, whose current students are soliciting funds by organizing a "telethon," the goal of which is to reach the greatest number of alumni possible and to bring them back to the flock (and remind them of their obligations). It is significant that these "telethons" have, until now, been crowned with an enormous success.

This accessibility is of course accompanied by a certain vulnerability, as I am within the reach of undesirables—potential thieves who use the telephone to verify if the coast is clear (hence the American incomprehension of the French *abonnés absents* system, where the caller is told there is nobody at that number for the moment), obscene phone callers, and so on. This is why, as a security measure, children are taught to answer the phone (and not to tell the truth) very early on.

The preceding implies that if I want to avoid these phone calls, my only recourse will be to have an unlisted number, which will cost me money. I can also install an answering machine, which does not really free me but allows me to choose the moment when I would like to respond. Indeed, if someone calls and leaves his or her telephone number or a message on my answering machine, it is only common courtesy to call that person back. The purpose of the answering machine, then, is to allow me to receive the calls that would have been lost in my absence rather than to avoid these contacts. It is therefore not unusual, on returning home, for me to check my machine first thing. And it is very likely, even if I do not admit it, that I would be somewhat disappointed if there were no messages, if no one had called in my absence. The meaning of the answering machine is often misunderstood by French people, who tend to feel insulted at having to speak to a machine. Here again, for a French person, the dividing line should remain clear between private and public life.

What leads me to bear the expense of an answering machine, aside from security measures (it is impossible to know if I am really at home or not), is the need to make myself available to all those "who never find me home," who "never manage to reach me," and who tell me this as a reproach ("You're hard to find"; "I called many times but could never find you"). They may also reproach me for being inaccessible because my line is always busy. In this case, I may be obliged to have two lines, two telephone numbers, both listed, or to install a "public" line and a "private" line (an unlisted number which I would give to only a chosen few). Similarly, as soon as my children are old enough to "spend hours" on the telephone, I will, if I have the means, install a line, so they will have their own number. If I cannot afford it, I will establish strict rules concerning the use of the telephone so that their calls do not restrict my own.

In other words, as an American, I will tend to consider the telephone as I consider the car, an indispensable means of overcoming the obstacles of distance and time. On this point, it is interesting to note that currently, as the "deregulation" of telecommunications has brought about continual revisions in rates, groups have formed to defend the right of the poorest segment of the population to have telephones, which the new rates would prohibit. The companies responded by offering "telephone vouchers," that is, special assistance to the indigent, following the model already adopted by the gas and electric companies, thus making the telephone an indispensable need, one of life's necessities. (In several cities, a system of protection connects old people living alone to the police or to volunteers.)

While unannounced visits are frowned upon in the United States, the telephone on the other hand makes me accessible to everyone, without distinction. Of course, if I receive a call at an unheard-of hour (after midnight), it had better be from a very close friend, someone who knows I am awake at that hour and whom I routinely allow to call me. I may tell someone to call me "any time," but it is with the expectation that he or she will not take me literally. Aside from these extremes, people can call me whenever they like between eight in the morning and ten or eleven in the evening. This does not bother me, insofar as I feel no remorse at picking up and saying "I can't stay on the phone right now" and that I will call back, or in asking that person to call me back. This will not anger the caller in the least, unless of course I always answer his or her calls in this manner and never call back.

From this perspective, it is not surprising that students or colleagues call me at home, maybe even more often than they do at my office (where I am much more difficult to locate, what with classes, meetings, seminars, forays into my colleagues' offices, etc.). Moreover, if students leave a message with the secretary or on my door, it is more polite for them to say that they will call back rather than ask me to call back by leaving their numbers. This quickly distinguishes the "naive" from the more experienced, who quickly learned that I will not "waste my time" trying to contact them to answer their questions.)

Long telephone conversations about "nothing important" are considered a waste of time and a sign of immaturity. Teenagers "spend hours on the phone" talking to friends whom they have just seen or who live across the street. For a long time, conversations among women were placed in this category by men who "had better things to do"; these conversations were the butt of "classic" jokes. If men had long phone conversations, they were supposed to be discussing more serious things and trying to resolve major problems such as the techniques for laying a carpet, analytical commentaries on a football game, metaphysical questions, the merits of a particular lake for fishing, and so on. Feminism has changed all that to some degree and has given those who like to "shoot the breeze" under the pretext of talking about work the freedom to do so unabashedly.

As an American adult, I do not call people "for no reason." I call my friends who live far away to find out how they are (and to maintain ties and friendship). I call my parents to make certain of their well-being and on holidays that we cannot spend together (Mother's Day and Thanksgiving seem to be the most important in this respect). Now and then I call members of my family with whom I have remained in contact in order to catch up on the latest events, to exchange news which great distances prevent us from hearing (if we do not write). Locally, I call friends to invite them to come to my house, in which case the conversation remains very short and is limited to making an appointment, or I call to ask for help, in which case the conversation is also very short, or at least lasts only the time necessary to explain the nature of the help requested and to obtain an answer.

These conversations "among friends" might seem abrupt to a French person. We should, however, see them as a mark of friendship rather than as a means of "getting rid of" someone. Indeed, when I see X, for dinner or for a visit, he gives me all his attention and a good chunk of his time. It would be indelicate and selfish of me to keep him on the phone for a long time, simply to chat; since he is my friend, I know the many things and people demanding his attention, and I am not going to retain him with useless calls, which, if they cause constant unjustified interruptions, might aggravate him or cause him to become impatient.

A television publicity campaign for the telephone company is very revealing on this point. We see people having the type of conversations that Americans are not used to having on the telephone, that is to say, "just for pleasure"; the refrain "Reach out, reach out and touch someone" invites Americans to consider the telephone as French people do. (I am sure, however, that this cultural overlap is purely by chance, that the telephone company's intention is not to promote a French custom but to multiply the number of calls by adding a new type of call to those already in existence).

# 7  "Minor Accidents"

A commercial on American television shows a mother and daughter (twelve or thirteen years old) trying to resolve the problem of a stain on a blouse. The daughter is frantic; her mother promises to do her best to help her. Thanks to a miracle detergent, the blouse is returned to its former beautiful state. In order to understand the depth of the crisis resolved by the detergent in question, one must know that the stained blouse does not belong to the girl on the screen but to her older sister, who lent it to her. The situation is serious enough for the mother to enter the picture, and for us to be relieved (and thankful for the magic detergent) when the blouse, unharmed, is put in its proper place just before the arrival of its owner, who, as it turns out, wants to wear it that very evening. The crisis has been averted; the heroines smile.

Things are not so rosy in the "Dear Abby" column, which millions of Americans read every day in the newspaper. The same problem often appears in many forms: "X borrowed my thingamajig, returned it damaged, and offered neither to replace it nor to repair it. What should I do?"

Are Americans frightened by their older siblings (the first case), or incapable of resolving the slightest problem (the second case)? The list of "adjectives" and of "explanations" can go on, according to one's tastes and culture. What interests me here is the fact that in both "cases" there was a "minor accident." In the first case, the "guilty" party knows what to do while in the second the "victim" does not know what to do, which indicates that an expectation was not met.

For a French person, it is likely that both cases would serve as additional proof of the "keen sense of proprietorship characteristic of Americans." But why lend one's property if one feels that way about it? It seems, here again, that the nature of the problem lies elsewhere.

Before going any further, however, it would be useful to review a few French cases of "minor accidents." Some of these cases are taken from personal experience. They seemed completely "normal" to the French woman in me but slightly "strange" to the anthropologist in me, who considered them with a voluntarily "foreign" eye.

F (a French woman), her husband, and her daughter, who are preparing to leave a party, are standing in the foyer saying goodbye. As she leaves, F has a "minor accident": while putting on her coat, her hand brushes against a small painting, which, dislodged by the movement, falls to the ground. The lacquered wooden frame breaks, but the damage is reparable. F says to her host, from whom she was just taking leave: "Oh, sorry, I had a little accident." Then, suddenly joking: "But what an idea to put a painting in such a place! My word, you must have done it on purpose!" Not knowing what to do with the little painting which she now has in her hands, she turns it over, probably to examine the damage, and cries out joyously, "Oh, you see, it must have already been broken, since it has been glued." Upon saying this, she points to a piece of sticky paper which appears to have nothing to do with the frame itself. Everyone present clearly sees this, but they all act if they hadn't noticed, and the host (who is French) hurriedly takes the painting from her and says "Don't worry about it, it's nothing, I'll take care of it." As F attempts to joke some more about the accident, her husband drags her toward the door, saying, "Listen, if you keep this up you'll never be invited here again." Everyone laughs. Exeunt all.

Not once did F offer to have the frame repaired. Rather, it seemed as if all her efforts tended toward minimizing the gravity of the accident by making a joke of it. She thus started recounting another incident: her daughter, when she was still a baby in her mother's arms, had unhooked a signed (she insists) plate from the wall behind her mother, and threw it on the floor. "Well that was a real catastrophe, I didn't know what to do with myself . . ." In other words, the "truly" serious incident, that of the valuable (signed) plate, was the fault of the baby (and at the same time not her fault, since she was a baby?). In comparison, the incident with the frame appears (or should appear?) negligible.

Does the comparison of these two incidents also imply that F is not responsible either? Like the baby? The fact that she did not offer to repair the frame (which would be a recognition of her responsibility) seems to indicate that this is a plausible interpretation of this comparison. Of course, we can say that F was so embarrassed that in the second case, as in the first, she "didn't know what to do with herself" and that joking was a way to hide her embarrassment. But one can just as easily be sorry or embarrassed, and joke around to relax the atmosphere, while at the same time offering to repair the damage.

While at a party at the home of friends of her friends, D, twenty-two years old, Parisian, spills red wine (a full glass) on the carpet. She grabs a small paper napkin to wipe it up. The friend who had invited her quickly returns from the kitchen with enough paper towels to really soak up the large quantity of wine; someone else brings salt. D, while her friend is cleaning, says, "My God, L (the host) is not going to be happy . . . but can you imagine. . . . That's the trouble with light-colored carpeting, it's so difficult to clean!" D made an effort, although insufficient, to repair the damage. But her commentary is strangely similar to that of F. The "victim" seems to be transformed into the truly responsible party, that is, into the person who is ultimately responsible for the accident: if the painting hadn't been placed there . . . if the carpet hadn't been chosen in such a light color . . .

Monsieur T, while visiting his son in the United States, discovers the existence of window shades, which are placed between the window panes and the curtains in the great majority of American homes and which serve to block out the sun. These shades are spring-loaded, which allows one to lower or raise them to any degree at will and thereby to adjust the quantity of light let in. In order to do this, one must learn to accompany the shade with one's hand, or else it winds itself up suddenly with a snap. The son demonstrates this for Monsieur T, insisting particularly on the fact that he must never release the shade and "let it roll up by itself" (which the French in the United States are endlessly tempted to do, even if they have been living here for more than twenty years, as I have). The next day, the son briefly reminds him of his instructions and only succeeds in exasperating Monsieur T ("Do you think I am a fool?"). A few days later, the son hears a snap, which sounds like a shot, followed by an exclamation. He runs over and finds his father in front of the window; as soon as he sees him come in, his father says, "This is horrible, you'd think you were in the devil's den. My word! Can't have a weak heart at your

place. . . . It's not surprising that Americans all go to psychia-
trists. . . . That gave me a terrible fright, and yet I did exactly as you
said, I don't understand what happened."

L, twenty-eight years old, from the Bordeaux region, shares an
apartment with V, approximately the same age, from Normandy. L
burns one of her good saucepans while V is out. Upon V's return, L
confesses, apologizes, and, in the course of her explanation adds,
"because, you know, for me, a good saucepan or a bad saucepan are
the same, because I'm not at all materialistic, I don't get attached to
objects." In other words, if this is considered an "accident," it is only
because it is V's nature to regret the loss of a simple saucepan, a mere
object.

M, from the Midi, lends his projector to S, who returns it,
jammed, with these words: "Your projector is strange, it makes a
funny noise." S later discovers a slide which is part of M's collection
wedged in the slide mechanism.

S, from the Basque coast, borrows R's car, brings it back the next
day, and asks with a sly smile: "Are you sure your car works well?
Because it stalled twice. Once, I was even stuck in the middle of the
road because I was trying to turn, and I was afraid a car would hit me."
R, who is S's friend, adds, upon relating to me this incident: "S is a
very nice guy, but he can't drive to save his life."

B, from Paris, returns the typewriter he borrowed from me, and,
wearing the mischievous smile of a naughty child who knows he will
be excused, tells me, "You know, your typewriter was very mean to
me, it must not like me very much because it was skipping letters
constantly. . . . I had to be very careful as I typed."

The preceding examples seem to indicate that French people do not
offer to repair things when there has been an accident. Yet this is not
the case. Among the cases I collected, offers to repair the damage were
just as common as those mentioned above. Thus L, who had already
burned V's saucepan, had also, at another time, accidentally broken a
hand-crafted pitcher which V had brought back from France. In this
case, L, who did indeed understand the sentimental value of pitchers
if not the material value of saucepans, offered, or rather promised, to
replace the broken object ("I'll buy you one exactly like that"). Over a
year later, V tells me, the pitcher had not been replaced, or even
mentioned.

This same V, G tells me, borrowed an electronic, programmable calculator to do "a few simple calculations." The calculations were apparently too simple for the delicate mechanism of the instrument because it became "mysteriously" blocked. V offered to share the cost of repairing it with G, thus implying that there must have been something wrong with the machine before she borrowed it (or else she would have offered to pay all the costs). According to G, the cost of repairing it turned out to be so astronomical that he preferred to buy another inexpensive calculator, "just in case." In the meantime, according to G, V never mentioned sharing the costs and never asked for news of the wounded calculator. The last I heard, G and V are still friends.

A variation on this case consists of saying what one would have liked to do, but did not do, to repair an accident. For instance, a white tablecloth which K borrowed from a friend for a holiday meal was irreparably stained. "I thought of buying a tablecloth to replace yours, but I didn't know what you'd like," says K, several years after the accident. The friend asserts that she has never been compensated and that it never put their friendship on the line.

Finally, there are certain cases in which the repair was made. Yet the comments differ depending on whether one talks to the person who caused the "minor accident" and repaired the damage or to the person who was the "victim." I have on occasion heard the former say things such as "I paid a great deal to have a worthless rug cleaned," whereas the latter, whose car was dented and repaired by the friends who had borrowed it made the following comment: "Of course, they paid for the repairs, but now the car is totally ruined."

We might conclude from the preceding examples that the French break everything and repair or replace nothing. Certain French people think so, and, as a result, "do not lend anything to anyone" and "do not ask anything of anyone," because "they never give it back in the state you lent it." As we know from having learned La Fontaine's fables, "Madame Ant is slow to lend \ The last thing, this, she suffers from."* But there are obviously many French people who do not hold this attitude, as is proven by the accident cases cited earlier. How then can we interpret the various ways in which the actors treated these

---

*From "The Ant and the Grasshopper," in A *Hundred Fables from La Fontaine*, trans. Philip Wayne (Doubleday).

accidents? As we have seen, the reactions ranged from playful jokes to reproachful jokes, and from reproachful jokes to disguised accusations. Offers of repair were not made, made but never followed up on, mentioned as something one had thought of, or else made and followed up on but to no one's satisfaction.

In other words, when I have a "minor accident," it is not really my fault. It is because an object was in a bad place (I might almost say "in my way"), because a carpet was too light to hide stains, because a machine was too delicate to function normally, because to have shades in a house is aberrant, and so on. In fact, I acted in all innocence and nothing would have happened if the others had correctly played their parts. It becomes clear that by joking and "taking things lightly," I place responsibility where it belongs, on the person who committed the error of poorly placing his painting, of choosing an insane color for a carpet, of buying an overly complicated calculator . . . and who, most of all, made the mistake of not sufficiently protecting his possession if he cared about it so much.

By pushing this logic to its extreme, I would say that when entertaining me, X runs the risk of having his good crystal broken if he chooses to use it ("accidents can happen") and that when lending me an object, he should warn me of its fragility. In fact, he should not lend, or put within my reach, an object which is fragile, and certainly not an object about which he cares a great deal. If he does this, X is obviously the one who should assume ultimate responsibility for the accident. Similarly, if I offer to repair or to pay for the damage ("tell me how much I owe you"), I have done my part, I have fulfilled my duty; it is up to X to request the necessary sum when required since I told him I would give it to him. Thus, I force the other to take responsibility for some of my acts, and in doing so I propose or reaffirm a relationship. If X refuses this relationship, he will never again invite me to his house or lend me anything more. And this does happen. But if X accepts the relationship, he reinforces it by placing more value on it than on the damaged object, as valuable as that object may be. Hence the "leave it, it's not important," which erases the accident. And as we more or less tacitly honor the same code, we each have a chance to be both victim and perpetrator of an accident, thus becoming linked to one another and affirming, sometimes against our wishes, the importance of these bonds.

Needless to say, an American would be completely baffled by such conduct. It is, in fact, this type of behavior that provokes the "Dear Abby" letters mentioned at the beginning of this chapter.

An informant described to me the "American general rule" as follows: "If I lend X my car, the minimum I can expect is that, before returning it, he will fill it with more gas than he consumed. If I lend him my car for a fairly long period, he will make a point of returning it to me in a better state than when I lent it to him (washed, waxed, vacuumed, etc.). He will not do this in order to point out my negligence but, in a sense, to repay me for my generosity. He will take responsibility for any necessary repairs, and I will hold him to this (unless it is an old wreck, in which case I would refuse to lend it to him so as to spare him some very predictable, but difficult to attribute, expenses)." Let us then look at some American cases, such as they have been reported to me.

At an elegant dinner, J breaks a crystal glass. She asks the hostess to lend her a glass of the same set, so that she can find a perfect replacement. The hostess honors her request.

P, fourteen or fifteen years old, meets a group of friends at D's house. They go to play basketball at the school basketball court and return, tired from the game, to D's house, where his mother serves them lunch. P, drawn without knowing why to a carafe on the buffet, picks up the stopper, which slips from his hands, falls back on the carafe, and chips it. P, confused, apologizes to D's mother for his clumsiness, and without hesitating offers to replace the carafe. P is over forty today, yet he remembers this scene very clearly. He remembers that at the very moment when he offered to replace the carafe he knew that he did not have, but would have to find, the necessary sum, and he also remembers that D's mother left him an escape route ("I'll let you know when I find one"), but not without her having expressed concern and regret over the accident. That is to say, according to him, D's mother was willing to be generous, but without diminishing P's responsibility.

A dinner with friends. M spills a glass of wine. His wife quickly runs to the kitchen, returns with the necessary products, and sponges up the wine—in short, does everything to repair the accident. M thanks his wife with a look of gratitude and apologizes for his clumsiness. Note: in this case, M's wife has repaired his clumsiness because she forms a couple with him and therefore shares responsibility for the accident, takes responsibility for it as well. This does not preclude the possibility that some couples have "sexist" habits, but it gives the gesture a deeper meaning, as is shown by the fact that the inverse is just as possible: a woman spills some wine and her husband tries to repair the damage (see the chapter on the couple).

An informal evening. Guests are seated on the carpet, their drinks by their sides. An accident quickly occurs: N spills a glass of tomato juice. The same efforts to clean it, as well and as quickly as possible, are made. N asks if his hosts have a carpet cleaning foam. They respond in the negative. N offers to pay the cost of the cleaning. "Thanks, but don't worry, we'll take care of it, no problem." The difficulty seems to be resolved. Yet later in the evening, on several occasions, N makes allusion to his clumsiness ("Don't give it to me, you know how klutzy I am"; "Oh God, this stain is looking at me"; "I feel so bad, such a beautiful carpet").

A meeting of the members of our block association, held at the house of one of my neighbors. The sofa and chairs are fitted with slip covers, the furniture with cloths to protect the wood, and the table with an oilcloth. Coffee and cake are served in paper cups and on paper plates. Everyone is relaxed, there is no chance of an irreparable accident, everything has been foreseen.

Another meeting, at the far more elegant home of one of my colleagues. C, who is about to place his glass of white wine on the coffee table in front of us, stops his gesture halfway and asks our host if the wooden table (modern, elegant) has been treated, "protected." Despite our host's affirmative response, another colleague comes to the rescue and passes C a wooden coaster from a small stack which had been discreetly placed on a table nearby. The glass of cold white wine will leave no trace of its dampness.

The recital of cases could go on indefinitely. Those which I have mentioned suffice to illustrate the implicit rules governing American interpersonal exchanges in case of a "minor accident." I will summarize them as follows:

1. If I borrow an object from someone, I have an obligation to return it in the very same state as when it was lent to me. If it is a machine that breaks down in my hands, I must repair it, so as to erase all traces of the mishap. (I don't do this in order to hide the accident, which I must mention in any case, but in order to return the object to its previous condition.)

2. If the damage is irreparable, I must replace the object by an identical one, no matter how much time and searching are required. I can, however, ask the owner of the object where it was purchased. I must not replace it by an "equivalent," which would mean brushing off as unimportant all the reasons for the owner's choice, or the meaning which a certain object has come to have for its owner. Nor can I replace the object by another similar—but more or less expensive—one (a glass for a glass, for example), because in both cases I would be suggesting that all that counts in my eyes is the price of the object.

3. If I have an accident at someone's home, the situation is even more delicate. If I have even slightly damaged a valuable object (an art object or one with sentimental value), I must be grieved by my clumsiness without finding any excuse for myself; I must immediately offer to take the object and to have it repaired (while showing that I know where to go and that I am not going to worsen the damage by leaving the object with nonprofessionals); I must insist on being allowed to do this, if only to relieve my feelings of guilt ("I feel so bad. I wouldn't be able to sleep"). If my host does not wish to signal the end of our relationship, he or she will, out of kindness, allow me to take the object with me, in order to "let me off the hook."

If the accident is of a common sort and not very serious, I must do everything in my power to repair the damage then and there, but I must be careful not to insult my host by offering to replace a common item or to pay the cost of cleaning a tablecloth, for instance, because in doing so I would be suggesting that I do not think he or she has the means to take care of it. In this case, I show that I take the accident seriously by mentioning it several times, by berating myself for my clumsiness, by making fun of myself—in short, by taking total responsibility for the accident.

All this might seem strange, if not "heavy-handed," to a French person. Why make such a fuss? Why put on such an act? Is this yet another example of American "hypocrisy" and "puritanism"?

It is nothing of the kind, of course. On the contrary, although their conduct may be completely different from that of the French people mentioned above (in fact it is exactly opposite), the Americans I have focused on sent a message very similar to that expressed by the French people. Indeed, when I (an American) borrow an object from X, I create or confirm a tie with X (I do not borrow things from just anyone). The care I take with this object will therefore be proportionate to the importance I place on my relationship to the person who lent it to me. Similarly, when I accidentally disturb a home to which I have been invited, my reaction will be interpreted as a conscious commentary on the relationship between my host and myself. If I do everything possible to clean a carpet, it is not for the sake of the endangered carpet (or because my host and I are "materialistic" because we are American) but out of respect for my host. In other words, our relationship does not presuppose that we will "weather difficulties" together (as it does in the French context); it presupposes a tacit pact between the borrower and the lender, the host and the guest, to preserve an equilibrium, without which all relationships of this kind would become impossible. For if I show little concern for something belonging to X which he has put within my reach or at my disposal (thereby trusting me), X has the right to feel wounded, scorned, and to refuse further dealings with me. Meanwhile, the expectation that one will honor this pact is so strong that any avoidance or refusal on my part risks leaving X bewildered, "not knowing what to do," just like the Dear Abby correspondents mentioned earlier. This is, in a sense, because for Americans it is not in the cards that others will behave in ways other than expected (without being criminals, louts, or other types with whom X would not maintain relations).

If my "accident" is really major and X refuses to allow me to free myself, as far as is possible, from my debt, X transforms this bond into a shackle, and I have no reason to maintain a relationship with someone so unconcerned with my feelings.

In many circumstances, intercultural misunderstandings spring from the fact that surface resemblances and behavioral similarities conceal profound differences in meaning. It is interesting to see here that the inverse is also true.

# 8   Obtaining Information

An American anthropologist summarized in these terms the feeling of disorientation he experienced on his first trip to Japan: "I was in a department store in Tokyo, in a true technological paradise which makes the United States seem like an underdeveloped country, and was tempted to buy all sorts of things. But I was completely lost, not knowing a word of Japanese. Suddenly in the back of this immense store, I noticed a sign on which the word "Information" was written in large letters and in English. I hurried over, and discovered that all the rest was written in Japanese."

I still do not know why this sign was in English, or what one had to do to obtain information in this department store, which obviously catered to foreigners (at least to English-speaking foreigners). But I am now convinced that there is a key to this apparent contradiction, since I have become aware of at least three ways of obtaining information, each very different from the next, according to the culture.

For instance, on Nukuoro, posting information for everyone to see was absolutely useless. We had a two-way radio which enabled us to communicate with the outside world, and thus to learn the exact date when the ship, the sole link between the island and the rest of the world, would arrive. On the "street" side of our verandah, in the very center of the village, we periodically posted notices containing all the available information about the predicted arrival of the ship in question. This information was written in the local language. We had decided to post this so that everyone in the village could have precise information (as the ship spent only a few hours in the lagoon every two months, it was very important for them to be able to foresee its arrival), and also so that we could avoid having constantly to repeat the same story. It was no use. People stopped in front of the sign, read it aloud, and then called us to verify that the ship was, in fact, coming. We quickly abandoned this method, having understood that the value of information, in this context, in no way related to its "factuality" (in our terms) but to its location in a network of interpersonal relationships.

In the United States, if you want any type of information, you pick up the phone and call the agency that is able to provide it. If you do not know whom to call, you ask one of the various agencies created for this purpose whom to call for the desired information. If all else fails, one can always ask the operator or inquire of the local newspaper, the local library, or even the police. Generally the response will be given in a friendly manner. If the person questioned does not know the answer, he or she will suggest other possibilities, other telephone numbers to call. The motto of the telephone directory in the United States is "Let your fingers do the walking." It is not unusual to hear, in a store for example, "we don't have any more, but you might find some at Y (competitor), or maybe at Z; other than that, I don't know who would have it."

This system seems very simple to Americans, and yet French people—even those who have lived in the United States for a long period of time—have trouble adjusting to it. Yet it is a matter neither of linguistic difficulty nor of one's attitude concerning the telephone (see the chapter on the telephone), or at least it is not only that. Rather, it seems that the French feel "overwhelmed" by the "mountain" of information "which one obtains in response to the slightest question"; also, they cannot understand being informed about competitors.

Americans claim to be completely baffled or defeated by the French system; they "resign themselves" to "wasting hours in order to obtain the slightest bit of information" and return home loaded with "horror stories" about the days they spent "running from one office to the next, without ever being able to obtain a satisfactory response." I believe it is clear that it is not "just" a matter of information.

In the United States, I am always struck by the abundance of detailed maps, whether printed, photocopied, or hand-drawn, which accompany invitations (I have one in front of me, drawn in a rather rudimentary fashion, which accompanied an elegant wedding invitation). Thus, in order to get to Jerry's house for the first time, all I need is his address and the map he gives me. Indeed, he may even have marked on the map, to help me, a colored line tracing the route leading to his door.

In the hospital, a system of colored lines on the floor leads me through wings and buildings to the ward I am seeking with no possible error. Wherever I go, I will be sure to find some type of map. In lieu of a map (while on the telephone, for instance), I will receive very precise directions ("Are you coming by car? Where are you coming from? Good, okay, go two miles south; at the third light after Fifth Street, turn right; continue west for about three miles, and you will come to a fork; bear to the right; turn left at the fourth street, and you will see two white houses and one yellow one; we're right across from the yellow one"). This presupposes that the person speaking and I have maps in our heads, on which we mentally trace the route. I finally learned, from sheer necessity, and after years of self-training, to give my address "American-style": "we are on the northwest corner of First and Madison." Even today, I secretly smile each time I hear myself say this. And if I want to provoke a smile of incomprehension or surprise, I have only to give the same directions to a French friend. But if I want the friend to find my house, I had better add, "coming from the campus, you walk down Madison until you come to First Street; cross First and it's the house on the righthand corner." I know I am not alone in performing these mental gymnastics; hence this essay.

When I (a French person) go to the post office in the United States to find out how to send my packages, I am informed of every possibility, even those I am not considering; I am given all sorts of information about special rates, the fastest means, the least expensive, the useless ("you'd be better off not sending it this way"). Of course, it is not because I am French that I receive such a response, but it is because I am French that I am struck (and sometimes overwhelmed) by the veritable flood of information, this labyrinth through which I am supposed to find my way. And this dizzying feeling hits me almost everywhere, whether I seek information about car rentals, train departures, different types of carpeting, tires, computers or screwdrivers, or about different flavors of ice cream.

In other words, when I, an American, ask for information, I expect to be presented with an entire spectrum of choices from which I can make my selection, just as I find my way on a map. When I enter a store, I want to have the freedom to browse as I please, to take the time "just to look." I will turn to the salesperson when I need supplementary information or help. Similarly, in the street, if I must ask passersby for directions, it is because I involuntarily lost my way by taking a wrong turn, or because I have come to an unfamiliar or unexpected place—in short, because I am lost. Many Americans make a point of never having to ask for directions, of always being able to "manage alone," which is why, in such circumstances, they do not mind looking like tourists by opening a map on the street. If I (an American) must ask my way, I will turn to anyone, because there are only two possibilities in my mind: either the person does not know and will simply tell me so ("sorry, I don't know"), or he knows and will give me as precise directions as anyone else. If I do not want to "waste" time, I will ask someone who is part of the neighborhood (someone mowing a lawn, or who works in a store, for example) rather than a passerby. In the same vein, for whatever information I may need, I will ask directly at the office I judge to be best qualified to answer me rather than ask my brother, my wife, or my neighbor.

What do I (a French person) do to obtain information? My first impulse is to turn to a person, to ask another person. Thus, for example, when it is a matter of finding an address, I will not hesitate (unless I am shy, but even then) to ask a traffic cop, and perhaps several people successively, for directions. I will even make a point of never being caught with a map in hand, "like a tourist." And if the directions are very complicated and the explanation very long, I will, in a sense, divide my route into segments and only concern myself with one segment at a time, thus addressing several passersby, one after the other.

Before trying to interpret this behavior, I would like to cite several cases that were reported to me by French informants.

"I am about to return to France for a visit of approximately one month. M, who has just spent one year in the United States, is returning home for good, but not until the end of the summer. It is now April. M asks if I would bring with me her thick winter coat, which she will not need until next winter in Paris. As she has no address in Paris, I must drop off the coat at her brother's house, in a Parisian suburb. The coat alone fills the only suitcase I am planning to bring for a one-month vacation. I therefore ask her why she does not send the coat by mail, by boat since it is not urgent, and directly to her brother's house. Answer: 'I'm afraid it will be too expensive by mail.

You see, J sent a tiny little package to her husband in Paris, and it cost her an arm and a leg.' 'But how did she send the book, air mail? by registered mail?' 'I don't know, in fact, it must have been air mail because I know it was urgent.' 'Listen, call the post office. They'll give you all the information you need, and if it's still a problem, I'll bring your coat.' M, who is nonetheless very intelligent, 'simply hadn't thought of it.' She went to obtain information at the post office, discovered that it was 'not at all expensive,' and decided to sent all sorts of other things which she would not need until her return to Paris." (The speaker is a French woman.)

"L, who did not know the best way to send all her baggage back to France, persisted in asking me questions which I was completely incapable of answering. I finally spent an entire afternoon on the telephone, with her by my side, gathering all the information she needed. The situation was all the more interesting as there was no linguistic difficulty (L was, on the contrary, quite proud of her English, often speaking English even to French people); nor was there any timidity on her part. Further, I had to ask her constantly for answers to the questions that the people at the other end of the line had asked me (expected date of shipment, weight, etc.). In the course of this afternoon, L often apologized for 'making me waste my time.'" (The French speaker is a man.)

"R [a Frenchman] woke me up at six in the morning. He was coming to Boston for three weeks (in January), had a long weekend free, and wanted me to find an interesting place where he could go for three days of relaxation in the sun. He told me he would call me back in two days. I then spent a good deal of time calling travel agencies and airline companies, and when R called back, I gave him all the information I had obtained. Each time, he asked me the same question: 'Do you know the place? Are there interesting things to do there? Because I have to relax, but I don't want to waste my only free weekend bored to death in the middle of nowhere.' In the end I told him, 'Listen, go to XX. I'm not familiar with the place but according to what I've heard, you won't be sorry.' In the end he wound up staying in Boston." (The speaker is a French friend of R's, and has been living in the United States for some time.)

It is possible that these situations were provoked by the strangeness of being in a foreign land, by a certain insecurity or ignorance due to the foreign context. They do, however, seem to be in keeping with a series of similar cases in which the need to turn to others cannot be explained by the incompetence one feels abroad. Rather, they pertain to the domain of requests for information in the street, which I mentioned earlier.

It seems that I choose which person to ask for information according to an implicit system of preferences, depending on the case. For instance, I (a French person) would prefer to turn to a person rather than to a map or a directory, which I would have to consult on my own. One need only glance at the information windows in train stations during vacation periods. At the Montparnasse station in Paris, for example, there is more than one way of obtaining information: in the concourse there are schedule boards on the walls, stacks of free timetables arranged in alphabetical order, directories on sale at tobacco stands; in the reservation and information room, there are directories and schedules for the public, brochures on all types of travel possibilities (group vacations, special rates, rent-a-car, etc.), in addition to the windows. The system of taking a number (and therefore of waiting) and that of using task-specific windows can be very slow. All this does not seem to discourage the throngs of people who patiently await their turn, numbers in hand. And the general information window is taken by storm. Few people consult the directories, schedules, and railway system maps, placed at the public's disposal (and therefore to be consulted alone). Often one comes only to verify with those who know officially what one already knows.

It therefore seems at first glance that French people do not fully trust themselves when it comes to gathering the information they need. Nor are they completely confident in the information givers, because "they're often wrong," "will say anything to get rid of you," or they "don't like to be bothered." Also, in order to give you information, these people need precise details from you ("I want to go on such and such a day, at such and such an hour." "Oh, I'm sorry but there is no train at that time"), and you yourself must propose the alternatives you would consider ("And the following morning, there is no train either?" "Oh yes, there are two in fact"). In certain circumstances however (a trip which is out of the ordinary), one is obliged to seek the help of these specialists.

Whom does one prefer to ask for information? According to my observations, a French person prefers to turn to a person rather than to a guide or to printed material, and to a person one knows rather than to a stranger. Indeed, if I am on the street with a friend and do not know my way but he "thinks he does," I will tend to follow my friend until the exhaustion from retracing our steps or my concern due to his hesitant look pushes me to ask my way from a stranger instead of repeating "Are you sure?" or "Where are you taking us?" The better I know the person in question, and the stronger our relationship, the more I will trust him or her, unless it is "common knowledge" that this person "never knows anything," "is always in the clouds," or "has no sense of direction."

I have often noticed this tendency to turn to others in the vicinity of vending and other machines. Still, at the train station, it is not unusual to see the following scene: someone faces an automatic ticket distributor, does not know how it works, but does not ask the person waiting to use the machine for help. Rather, he or she will say aloud, as if talking to the machine, "How on earth does this thing work?" thereby indirectly calling for help on the person next in line, who at that point will intervene (to do so without having been invited, even indirectly, would be an intrusion). I remember, on this point, having witnessed a marvelously absurd scene a few years ago, on the main street of La Rochelle. A small group in front of a bank machine caught my eye; I approached, all ears. In the center, a sixty-year-old woman was unsuccessfully attempting to withdraw money. Several people, in turn, tried to help her; they took her card, and asked her this question which I will never forget: "What was your secret code again?" And the woman answered, and the card passed from hand to hand, in an expression of trust which filled me with nostalgia.

In the same way, a French person, as opposed to an American, is often reluctant to read the instructions accompanying a new acquisition and prefers to ask someone close to him or her "how it works." We can even reach the extreme of "I just bought a . . . like yours; come show me how it works." In addition, there is often a member of the family (not necessarily an adult) who develops an unusual taste for reading instructions and to whom the other members defer ("Ask Jeannot, you know very well I don't know these things").

The preceding suggests that when I (a French person) ask for information, I am, in a sense, delegating power. I temporarily put myself in someone's else's hands, I undertake to follow his or her directions. This is why I will not ask just anyone.

I prefer to be in a face-to-face situation rather than on the tele phone (which inspires less confidence since I cannot see the person to whom I am speaking). In the street, I would prefer a traffic cop (someone whom one has to trust) or, if there is no officer, "someone who inspires confidence," that is to say, someone whom I will very quickly have judged (by demeanor, age, clothing) to be trustworthy. But my preference will be for someone I already have confidence in (who, for example, has accompanied me or given me information before). This can lead me to the extreme case of blind trust, where I refuse to believe that the person who gave me information was wrong, even if it entails going around and around the same block with no luck ("But I don't understand, it should be here").

This means that on asking for information from someone, I enter into a system of exchange of which we, the person I ask and myself, implicitly know the rules. In asking my question, I make a choice, and, if only for a brief moment, the person I select becomes the chosen one, a special person. One could even say that I am honoring a person by asking this person for information, since I do not place my trust in just anyone. In asking for information, I affirm the existence of a relationship. In exchange, the person interrogated will do "everything possible" to answer, that is, to be deserving of my trust. Sometimes, my question may reverberate through a whole series of persons: if X, whom I have just asked for information, does not know the answer, X will not just tell me "I don't know" but, more often, "I don't know, but wait, I'll ask Y who must know." Y will ask Z, and so on; I may regret having asked the question, but I must keep still and await the answer, even if it ends up taking too much time (this happened to me in a colleague's office at a Parisian university). On the street, it can happen that the person I ask for information will in turn stop another person. Similarly, in a store, the question may bounce back and forth and even disappear into the back room. In such a case, it would be impolite to leave without awaiting a response, having put into motion a system with which I should be sufficiently familiar so as not to make use of it if I do not intend to respect it.

If the person asked wishes to refuse the exchange, he or she will respond "I don't know," and in this case, unless all sorts of excuses are added ("I'm sorry," "I'm not from the area"), I will tend to consider this response, to a certain extent, as a rejection of my advances and will be taken aback. If, on the contrary, the person tries to answer, he or she is undertaking to fulfill the role with which I have entrusted him or her, which consists of "taking charge," of "taking care of me," if only for an instant. This explains why two persons asking for the same information in an office, a post office, or a bank, for example, will be treated differently. Although on the surface the situations seem identical, they have each communicated something different through their way of asking the question (their tone of voice, their gaze, etc.); thus, each one has or has not put him- or herself in the hands of the other (hence the difficulties met by foreigners).

But the exchange does not stop there. When a person gives me the information requested, I in turn undertake to respect the implicit rule, which is to take this information as true, even if it seems a bit odd. Thus, if I am on the street, I must walk in the direction that has been indicated to me for at least a short while, or else I am obliged to play some sort of game (linger in front of a store window, make a gesture indicating that I forgot something or that I made a mistake) to show that I have a good reason for not following the instructions immediately, a reason for which I alone am responsible. Otherwise, I risk offending the person I asked (and violating the implicit agreement) and sometimes even risk prolonging longer than I should that person's sense of obligation toward me. Indeed, if I do not immediately turn right as I was told to do, but continue straight, a voice from behind me may set me on the right track, or the person may even run after me to correct my error.

The obligation to play a role in this system of exchange can go so far as to push certain people to give information even if they are not qualified to do so, thus signifying that it is more important to answer (and thus to accept the relationship proposed) than to answer correctly. This situation has one very important implication for the person asking for information: as soon as I turn to someone, I am no longer responsible for myself; I have, in a sense, delegated this responsibility, and consequently the responsibility for my actions, to another person. Therefore if I make a mistake, if I commit an error, the responsibility falls on the other person's head, the person who gave me "wrong information." This explains why one hears, as a valid excuse and in all sorts of contexts, "they gave me the wrong information," "I was told that," "No one told me that," and so on.

In the United States, where self-sufficiency is prized, "not to need anyone" is a very desirable goal. In French, on the other hand, the expression sounds more like a reproach. The implicit notion is that you never give someone else the chance to do you a favor. In other words, to admit to needing someone, for example, by asking for a favor or information, is to give meaning to the other's existence, to affirm his or her importance. Thus, if I carry this logic to its limit, I can say that by asking someone for information, I give him or her the opportunity to do me a favor, but that someone who is never asked for anything, not even information, has a very sad existence, cut off ("voluntarily" is implied) from others.

Here we see how requesting a favor falls into the same category as requesting information, and we can now understand the ease with which a French person asks another "to do him a favor." I am much more aware of this since I have been living abroad. Just as M, whom I mentioned earlier, had not found it strange or out of place to ask her friend to carry a thick winter coat in her summer suitcase, so I have had many opportunities to verify that we seem to find it quite normal to ask for this type of small favor. And of course the closer the person, whether family or friend, the more I put him or her to use.

Thus, when I want certain French books, rather than order them from a bookstore in France, I first think of asking someone in France to send them to me (which forces that person to buy them, package them, go to the post office in his or her free time to send them, pay for all these costs, and most of all, to keep all of this in mind). Similarly, the first time I entered a certain bookstore in La Rochelle, where I was spending only a few weeks, and spoke to the young clerk about books, he asked me, when I returned to the United States, to let him know what books of importance were being published in all fields, and to send him copies of some of them. Of course I never did it, and he probably forgot his request as soon as I left the bookstore. But what is significant is that he would have made such a request, that he would not seem to find it extraordinary, or difficult for me to fulfill.

I also carried, for the brother of a friend, a package which the brother, who didn't live in Paris, had to come and pick up. Friends have brought me books, and I always count on my brother to send me all kinds of things connected with my research. A friend of mine (French) had one of his friends, whom he was to meet at a conference and who lives in the same city that I do, bring me a manuscript (a photocopy, and therefore nothing valuable), whereas an American would have put it in the mail. I myself returned the manuscript in person.

Certain requests arrive at the last minute before a departure, requiring frantic running around in order to honor them. These types of requests would obviously never be questioned in the French context, whereas an American would simply say "I'm sorry, I don't have enough time," "I'm sorry but I can't possibly do it." On this subject, I still remember with amusement the distress of a colleague who had just received a telephone call from his mother (in Paris), on the eve of his own departure (for Paris): she asked him to bring back a tube of suntan cream with PABA, which was, at that time, "nowhere to be found in France." So, he quite "naturally" turned to me.

We (French) may complain to third parties about these requests, especially if we turn to them for help—as my colleague had been "forced" to do by his ignorance of suntan creams—but we always try to honor such requests. Only the strength of the bonds thus established or maintained can explain the use, which some people avoid on all other occasions, of the transatlantic telephone for this type of favor. If someone asks a favor of me, I will do everything I can to honor the request (go way out of my way, waste a great deal of time, spend money), thus demonstrating that I am at the disposal of the person who asked (that I would not do it "for just anyone" is implied).

We might think that this is a special case, intercontinental messages rendered necessary by distance or by a lack of certain products. But the same situation is just as common in France, though less easily pinpointed. The request may sound less urgent: "The next time you go there, could you bring me . . . ?"; "If you're in the neighborhood, would you mind going to . . . ?"; "If you're around there, would you go see if . . . ?" They are, nonetheless, treated just as seriously.

When a small favor is performed, the person who requested it often behaves in a manner which surprises, and sometimes upsets, Americans. Suppose, for instance, I ask X, a friend, to go out of his way and "stop by the bakery" before coming to my house, where several of us are having dinner. X agrees to do this and arrives at my house very late. He apologizes, explaining that he realized that he "didn't have a penny" and had to stop by the bank. It was closed. He therefore used the bank machine, which swallowed his card. He then went to "his" baker (who knows him and can give him credit), which is not exactly on the way. He buys the bread I need, after having waited in line because it was near closing time. Upon leaving the bakery, he finds he has received a parking ticket because, in his haste, he parked illegally.

It is very likely that I will respond to this animated account with something such as: "You shouldn't have gone to so much trouble. You should have dropped the whole thing; I would have made rice . . ." Am I saying that X "did all this for nothing?" Clearly, X went through all this because, in asking him a favor, I was implicitly asserting that I "was counting on him," and because by choosing to ask him for a favor, I was suggesting the strength of the bond uniting us, which allowed for such a request.

In this case, my "you should't have"-type response (*tu n'aurais pas dû*) might seem cruel, since it seems to nullify all his efforts in one fell swoop and to refuse them all importance. In saying this, therefore, I may seem ungrateful or completely oblivious to his efforts. This is how many Americans told me they interpreted such a response (which some French people admitted "got on their nerves").

In fact, my (French) response has several possible meanings, depending on my manner of asking the favor. Reference to the initial request is sometimes made in the conversation following X's explanation. Thus, I could say: "But I told you 'only if you were passing by' (or 'if you think of it'); you shouldn't have gone to so much trouble!" Meaning: "You blew my request out of proportion, you are in the process of transforming a simple small favor into a huge debt, an obligation inconsistent with the nature of the request." But if, as I said earlier, X is my friend, this interpretation is probably not correct.

The phrase "you shouldn't have" does not indicate that I am unloading my responsibilities toward X, that I am minimizing his efforts. Rather, what I am saying is equivalent to "You went to a great deal of trouble and are thereby showing me the importance you place on our relationship; I want to show the same, in turn, by placing more importance on your well-being and your presence than on preparing a balanced meal, the absence or presence of bread, or the minor efforts I would have had to make to replace the bread."

X, in any case, fully understands the message implicit in "you shouldn't have," since he quickly reassures me that he is telling me all this only to explain his lateness (which otherwise could be insulting), that I shouldn't worry about it, that it was entirely his fault, how silly of him to find himself in such a position, penniless. . . . And it becomes another "good story" for us to share.

In other words, X's efforts and my protests affirm the same thing: the priority we give our relationship. Of course, this can easily serve as a cover-up and veil the exploitation of one of the parties. But such a case does not concern me here, since it falls within the realm of psychology, and not (or at least not directly) of cultural analysis.

The meaning I place on "you shouldn't have" (and other equivalent phrases) is confirmed by the fact that I will turn to X again for another favor, and he to me. (Let us underline, in passing, that we are not talking about the formal "Oh my dear, you should never have done it"—*Oh mon cher, vous n'auriez jamais dû*—used to welcome a ritual gift, which also corresponds to the American "You shouldn't have".)

If there is no preexisting relationship, I am not in a position to ask a favor, unless I thereby wish to establish one. I do not ask "anything of anyone, just like that." And if I am wrong about the nature of our relationship and thus ask for more than it allows, the manner in which the person will perform (or not perform) this "small" favor will make it clear. I will then know if I was "wrong about" him or her.

Only from this perspective can we easily understand the abundance of "small favors" which the French ask of each other, the number of cases in which they leave objects behind ("you'll send it to me"), in which they entrust friends with packages to give to other friends, or in which they call someone at the other end of the country, simply to ask him or her to call the office to let them know that their plane will be late (when it is eight in the morning and would be just as easy to call the office directly). In short, it is only from this perspective that we can understand the number of cases in which the most direct line between the world and myself passes through a third point.

This chapter might seem to contradict the one on friendship, in which I suggest that among French friends, the asker does not ask, but the friend offers. Yet this is not a contradiction: I do not hesitate to ask for "small favors," such as information. But when it is a matter of a "real" favor, a large favor, asking my friend to do it for me would be the equivalent of imposing it on him or her, since in the name of friendship he or she cannot refuse. In these cases I wait for my friend to offer.

It is interesting to note that the inverse is true for an American. I can ask what I like of my friends, who can refuse without hurting our friendship. But I will ask for information on the street or for "little favors" only if I cannot do otherwise, as a last resort so to speak. For such purposes, there are specialized bureaus, detailed printed instructions, tourist guidebooks, and an entire sector of the economy dedicated to the creation of more and more "services," some of which are most original: for a "reasonable" fee, I can hire a specialist to reorganize my entire office, my files, my old papers; I can send a "bellygram" on a friend's birthday; I can deposit all sorts of loose objects to be packaged and mailed in a "mail shop"; and so on. Thanks to the computer, the sources of information and services border on the infinite.

Here again, in a domain which seems most banal—requesting information—Americans and the French have profoundly different expectations. If I could summarize all of the preceding, I would say that when I ask for information, I (an American) want to obtain as many particulars as possible, which I will combine to my liking, whereas I (a French person) prefer to express my wishes and let others provide me the information which will allow me to satisfy them. It now becomes clear that in the first case what I need most is correct information, whereas in the second what I need most is someone to count on.

# Conclusion

All that precedes is just a beginning. Why stop here, why conclude? And how? This book has meaning only insofar as it is an opening. I wrote it only to invite others to try this path to the other, to invite them to start their own fascinating turtle hunt, knowing that the turtles will always rest upon still more turtles.

This means that this book is by definition incomplete, is intentionally incomplete, assuming that it is even possible for it not to be so.

Indeed, for cultural analysis to be effective, for it to transform a wound into fascination with the other, it must not be merely read but, rather, performed, practiced ceaselessly; it must become second nature, which implies, above all, that I must be prepared not to question my "self" ("I" would no longer exist in this case) but to examine my premises, each time my encounter with the opaque, the foreign, requires that I do so. Luckily, most of the time, my culture can "live with" the other culture, as there is no contradiction between our premises but rather peaceful coexistence, if not necessarily unity. This means that it is only when there is a clash, interference between our "natural" behaviors, opposition between our "invisible verities," that we must become aware of the relative nature of our truths if we wish to understand the source of our differences and that we must, at the same time, compel ourselves to enter the logical universe of the other through an enormous effort of the imagination.

At first glance, the experiment appears reassuringly simple. This is true until the moment I become fully conscious of the fact that what I am demanding of myself is a very complex mental exercise: indeed, in order to understand the other through cultural analysis, I must, at least temporarily, accept that my truth is precisely that, "my" truth, that it is not absolute truth, but a relative truth (all of which is easier said than done). At the same time I must become able to conceive that the "aberrant" behavior that wounds me (and incites me to defend myself, to deny, to condemn the other) may be informed (and thus formed) by the truth of the foreigner, of the other, that is to say, what he or she considers to be not "his" or "her" truth but "the" truth.

In other words, I expect my readers either to reject this type of analysis, reproaching it for not being all that it is not and does not pretend to be, or to enter the door that this book wants to open by taking a new look at their own experience of cultural misunderstandings in the light of this type of analysis. In this case their main concern will be not to "verify" the value of my texts (are they "representative?") but to confirm, refine, enrich, or contradict the results of this analysis in the light of other texts subjected to the same type of analysis; not to show that I am right or wrong (which should not be important to them, just as it is not important here) but to confirm or invalidate the value of cultural analysis as an effective method for the understanding of foreigners, as a personal practice in one's contact with that which is foreign, opaque, shocking, wounding; as a necessary and urgently needed practice in a world without borders, in which the foreigner is my neighbor, my friend, my lover, my child.

For those readers who reject this kind of analysis, I can only accept the failure of my attempt to seduce them. I know of no other way to reach them. For the others, I will have only played the role of a catalyst. Indeed, these people have long been seeking, though perhaps unconsciously, to understand; they travel, open their homes to otherness, make the disjunction familiar. For these people, cultural analysis will be a valuable tool. This tool does not belong to me: I am merely transmitting it, with instructions for use.

In the meantime, supposing that I am ready to try my hand at cultural analysis, will this effort automatically eliminate conflicts and misunderstandings? Why should I attempt to understand if the other makes no effort? Doesn't this mean I am giving in to the other, denying my own culture? Is awareness enough to resolve conflicts? Is awareness the equivalent of changing? Must I force myself to change? Why? What should I do if I cannot manage to do so?

These questions, and others I will mention later, are not empty questions which I am simply posing rhetorically. They were asked of me (sometimes with the urgency of despair), I have asked them my-self, and I consider them to be very serious. Indeed, why change that which allows me to function perfectly in my own culture? Why risk alienating myself in my homocultural relationships?

It is important to remind ourselves here of the difference between psychoanalytic analysis and cultural analysis. Indeed, psychiatric treatment and psychoanalysis should allow me to become reintegrated in my society, to be no longer alienated from my culture, to learn or to relearn my cultural premises without naming them, to eliminate what I consider (or what others consider) to be "difficulties" in my homo-cultural relationships.

Cultural analysis would therefore seem to create problems for me in precisely those areas where I have none (or I think I have none)—in my relationships with individuals of my own culture, the very same people who understand me "automatically," who share my idea of what is "natural." All this to understand foreigners? Wouldn't this result in lack of balance and in threat? In other words, I am willing to see a psychiatrist, if need be, if I have problems, if "something's not right." But why reexamine myself when I am comfortable in my skin, when I suffer from no psychic disorders, when I am at home like a fish in water, when the only difficulties in my relationships are created by foreigners who "don't understand anything," who are "impolite," "uncultured," "stubborn," "unadapted," "unadaptable," and so on? How can I keep my identity and lose it at the same time? And in the name of what?

The fear of losing oneself through this type of analysis, of invol-untarily changing and in an unknown direction, is common, whether it is recognized or not; but it is mostly characteristic of those who are monocultural. It is possible and in fact even usual for an individual to live for years in a foreign country, to speak another language fluently, but to remain essentially monocultural. It is even possible to be an anthropologist and to remain (more or less uncon-sciously) monocultural. This should be reassuring. Indeed, one cannot be rid of one's culture at will. Moreover, I do not believe I could rid myself of my cultural premises even if I wanted to, because it is not a matter of changing what I believe in but of recreating what I am, independent of what I have made myself. No matter how hard I try, I will always react in a manner that is "natural" to me. Indeed, as soon as I "let down my guard," this is exactly what happens. (We should rather say "what's culturally bred in the bone will come out in the flesh.")

Just as when I learn another language, I do not lose my mother tongue (though I may become a bit rusty), so understanding another culture can in no way threaten me, lessen me, or make my own culture disappear. But by making me aware of my difference, it may allow me to accept that of the other, to become enriched thereby. One important warning: if I emigrate to a foreign country, I can adapt to my adopted culture, but my cultural premises will not change, even though my adaptation may take the form of great superficial changes (I will return to this). But no matter how great my efforts, I cannot prevent the crossbreeding of my children's cultural premises unless I raise them within four walls, so to speak, with no contact with anyone from another culture (their mother or father, for example). Even in this case, however, I cannot change the fact that my children will have premises profoundly different from my own, since, as far as I know, there is no society (including the one from which I come) which "naturally" raises its children in this way. But short of bringing in moral arguments which have no place here ("we must understand each other," "let us love our foreign brothers and sisters," etc.), why would I choose to become "fascinated" with intercultural understanding when other "fascinating" topics beckon, topics which do not require me to "bend over backwards" questioning myself? For one reason and one reason alone, and this reason is clear, selfish, harsh, and convincing: sooner or later, no matter where I go in today's world, even if I stay at home, it is nearly impossible for me not to be a foreigner in turn, for me not to be opaque to someone who matters to me, who attracts me, whom I love, marry, give birth to, or with whom I simply want to do business. The practice of cultural analysis, as I have presented it here, is thus my system of preventive measures against possible injuries in interpersonal relationships—voluntary or involuntary—my way of pouring balm upon or of healing very real wounds, and therefore my passport to the liberating adventure of intercultural experience. Like any skill (flying a plane, being good in math), I derive from it a feeling of power over the unknown and of pleasure in entering this unknown.

As the unknown has no limits, this book can be no more than a beginning, a prologue; and this conclusion cannot conclude, since,

for whoever is still reading (why worry about the others?), this conclusion can be but an introduction. As the writer of this book, I must
make a choice: either I share this "introduction" with all the in-
completeness it, by definition, implies, or I wait to have analyzed
"everything" before writing, and therefore never write. The choice I
have made is no mystery.

To underline the extent to which this voyage is not, for me, termi-
nated or terminable, I would like to indicate other misunderstandings
which call for analysis and which I have only begun to examine. I will
then venture to interpret the main points resulting from the analyses
already discussed.

Money. Someone should talk about money. For a French person, the
face of an American could easily be replaced by a dollar sign. A sign of
"incurable materialism," of arrogance, of power, of "vulgar," unre-
fined pleasure . . . the list goes on. I have never read a book about
Americans, including those written with sympathy, which did not
speak of the "almighty dollar"; I have never had or heard a conversation about Americans which did not mention money.

Foreigners often discover with "horror" or "repulsion" that "everything in the United States is a matter of money." Indeed, one need
only read the newspapers to find constant references to the price of
things. Thus, a fire is not a news item but an entity (natural or
criminal), the dimensions of which are calculated by what it has
destroyed—for example, "a row of two-hundred-thousand-dollar
homes." In fact, if it is at all possible to attach a price to something, as
approximate as it may be, that price will surely be mentioned. Thus, a
French woman became indignant toward her American brother-in-
law: "He showed us the engagement ring he had just bought, and
he just had to give us all the details about the deal he got in buying the
diamond. . . . Talk about romantic!" I cannot even count the
number of informants who had similar stories to tell ("I was admiring
the magnificent antique pieces in his living room, and do you know
what he did? He gave me the price of each piece, with all kinds of
details I hadn'd asked for. I felt truly uncomfortable . . . really . . ."').
Many French informants claimed to be shocked by the "constant
showing off," the "lack of taste typical of nouveaux riches" and added,
some not in so many words, "As for me, you know, I am truly repulsed
by money."

On the other side, many Americans expressed surprise at the frequency with which French people spoke about money, only to say that "they weren't interested in it" ("so why talk about it?"), or at the frequency with which they say "it's too expensive" about all types of things. Some find the French to be "cheap" ("They always let you pay") or "hypocritical" ("Why, then, do the French sell arms to just anyone?"), too respectful of money to trifle with it, or too petty to take risks. The list of adjectives hurled from either side on this topic seems particularly long.

Yet a brief examination of certain ethnographic details left me puzzled. For instance, what is the American article, about the forest fire that destroyed the row of two-hundred-thousand-dollar homes in California, really saying? Living in the United States, I know that a house worth two hundred thousand dollars in California is far from a palace; on the contrary. Thus, if I took the price quoted literally, I would misinterpret the article as meaning that the fire had destroyed a row of quite ordinary houses—in which case the mention of the "price" is uninformative, uninteresting, and useless. Therefore, what this article conveys, by talking about hundreds of thousands of dollars, is the fact that the fire destroyed very valuable homes. This meaning is also conveyed by the use of the word "homes," which connotes individuality and uniqueness, rather than "houses," which suggests plain buildings. The mention of the price, therefore, carries meaning of a different nature: I think that this "price" serves only as a common point of reference; it does not represent the true monetary value but a symbolic value which can be grasped immediately by anyone reading this article. A French equivalent would be a reference to the period ("from the seventeenth century") with no mention of the state of the building.

Similarly, it is difficult to take the example of the engagement ring literally ("I'm a tightwad"; "I'm not romantic"); it is more comprehensible if we interpret it as a message with a different meaning. For the American in question, having obtained a discount in no way altered the true value of the diamond or the symbolic value of the gesture; this "feat" probably made the gesture even more significant because of the time and attention devoted to it (the worst gift is one that demands no effort) and probably earned him the admiration and appreciation of his fiancée.

The study of cases in which money is mentioned would require an entire book, which is why I did not address the issue in one chapter. I will content myself merely with raising the question here and will indicate the general orientation of my interpretation.

The striking thing is that money is charged with a multiplicity of meanings in American culture, that it has attained a level of abstraction difficult to imagine elsewhere. Money represents both good and bad, dependence and independence, idealism and materialism, and the list of opposites can go on indefinitely, depending on whom one speaks to. It is power, it is weakness, seduction, oppression, liberation, a pure gamble, a high-risk sport; a sign of intelligence, a sign of love, a sign of scorn; able to be tamed, more dangerous than fire; it brings people together, it separates them, it is constructive, it is destructive; it is reassuring, it is anxiety-producing; it is enchanting, dazzling, frightening; it accumulates slowly or comes in a windfall; it is displayed, it is invisible; it is solid, it evaporates. It is everything and nothing, it is sheer magic, it exists and does not exist at the same time; it is a mystery. The subject provokes hatred, scorn or impassioned defense from Americans themselves, who are constantly questioning themselves on the topic.

I believe that one association remains incontestable, no matter how much resentment it provokes. Money symbolizes success. It is not enough to have money to be admired, but quite the contrary; there is no excuse for the playboy who squanders an inherited fortune. To earn money, a lot of money, and to spend it, is to give the most concrete, the most visible sign that one has been able to realize one's potential, that one has not wasted the "opportunities" offered by one's parents or by society, and that one always seeks to move on, not to stagnate, to take up the challenge presented in the premises shaping the education of children (see the chapter on parents and children).

As a result, money has become a common denominator. It is supposed to be accessible to all, independent of one's origins. And if it creates classes, it also allows free access to these classes to whoever wants to enter. (Let's not forget that we are talking here about "local verities," about cultural premises, and not about social realities.) Money is therefore the great equalizer, in the sense that the highest social class is, in principle, open to everyone, and that while those who are born into this social class have definite advantages, they must nonetheless deserve to remain there, must "prove themselves." And the newspapers are filled with enough stories of poor people turned millionaires to reinforce this conviction.

From this perspective, it is understandable that one does not hide one's success but displays it, shows it off. By making my humble origins known, by displaying my success, I am not trying to humiliate others (although it is possible that I, personally, am a real "stinker"), but I am showing others that it is possible, I am encouraging emulation through example, I am reaffirming a cultural truth: "if I can do it, you can do it." Hence the constant copresence of dreams and success, that is to say, the constant reaffirmation that the impossible is possible, and that attaining the dream depends solely on me. The logical, and ironic, conclusion to all this is the essentially idea-listic significance of money in American culture, which does not exclude its "materialistic" utilization.

I do not believe that the misunderstanding between the French and Americans concerning money can be resolved by performing a parallel analysis of the meaning of money in French culture, not because money is not a concern for the French, but because I believe that what Americans express through money is expressed by the French in another domain.

From this brief analysis, I will reiterate three points. The first is that money in America serves as a common point of reference, a shortcut for communication, a means of defining a context that is recognizable by all and comprehensible no matter what one's financial situation may be. The second is that it is not in bad taste to recount one's triumphs, one's success in this domain, whether it is a matter of having obtained a half-price diamond or of having accumulated a veritable fortune, insofar as this in no way implies that I wish to put down others, that I am conceited, and so on, characteristics which depend not on money but on my personality. And the third is that money is accessible to all, makes possible upward mobility, that is to say, access to any class.

To the extent that these three points I just made are not "true" for French culture—and that they might in fact provoke "real repulsion"—one must look in a realm other than that of money for what carries the same message. I did this, constantly testing new hypotheses which I was then forced to reject. I finally felt that I had found it. I know that my hypothesis will seem scandalous to many French readers, that my interpretation will be controversial. I would nonetheless be happy if it managed to provoke a debate and thus to draw attention to the urgency of cultural analysis as a practice. I am ready to accept any other interpretation which seems more convincing than my own, if it respects the rules of cultural analysis (and not those of psychological, historical, economic, philosophical, or sociological analysis, the value of which I do not reject, but which pertain to another domain).

The repulsion with which many French people react to the "bad taste" of Americans who "brag about their wealth," "show off their money," and so on closely resembles the disgust with which many Americans speak of the "bad taste," the "vulgarity" of French people who "brag about their sexual exploits," "are proud of their sexual successes," which is a subject reserved by Americans for the "un-civilized" world of locker rooms, for the special and forced intimacy of these dressing rooms for athletes. (Although the expression "locker-room talk" traditionally evokes male conversation, it is just as applicable today to female locker-room talk.) The repugnance on the part of "tasteful" Americans to speak in public about their successes with men or women or their sexual "conquests" is interpreted, among the French, as additional proof of American "puritanism," whereas the French "modesty" concerning public conversations about money would tend to be interpreted by Americans as a type of French "puritanism."

This reciprocal accusation of "bad taste" led me to wonder if what was true for financial successes and conquests in American culture was not true for seduction, for amorous conquests, for sexual successes in French culture.

While it is not looked on favorably, in France, to show off one's money or titles, one may speak of one's amorous conquests without shocking anyone (unless one does it to belittle others with one's superiority, to insult them, etc., in which case it is not the subject that is important but the manner in which a particular person makes use of it). We have, in France, a great deal of indulgence and admiration for the "irresistible" man or woman, for "charmers" large and small of both cases. Seduction is an art which is learned and perfected.

Like money for Americans, amorous seduction is charged with a multiplicity of contradictory meanings for the French, depending on the person to whom one is speaking and the moment one raises the topic. Nonetheless, if a (French) newspaper article defines a particular person as *séduisante*, the term does not refer to indisputable characteristics but to a category recognizable by all, to a common point of reference, to a comprehensible descriptive shortcut. (It is interesting to note that the American translation of *séduisant* would be "attractive," a word which, as opposed to the French, evokes identifiable and predictable characteristics. The word *seductive*—not an adequate translation—evokes manipulation and the negative connotations attached to taking advantage of naïveté.)

Seduction, as I have said, is an art for the French. It is not enough to be handsome or beautiful to seduce; a certain intelligence and expertise are necessary, which can only be acquired through a long apprenticeship, even if this apprenticeship begins in the most tender infancy. (Thus, an ad for baby clothing, a double spread in the French version of the magazine *Parents*, shows the perfect outfit for the "heartbreak girl" and for the "playboy"; this is an indication of the extent to which this quality is desirable, since I assume the ad is geared toward the parents who provide for and teach these babies, and not toward the babies themselves.) It is therefore "normal" for me to be proud of my successes, for me to continually take up the challenge of new conquests, for me never to rest on my laurels, for me not to waste my talent. It is therefore not in "bad taste" to talk about it (bad taste and seduction are, in a sense, mutually exclusive in French). What is more, I can "freely" share my secrets and my "reflections" on the subject of men or women—a topic I have thoroughly mastered.

Like money for Americans, seduction for the French may be the only true class equalizer. In fact, one of the greatest powers of amorous seduction is precisely the fact that it permits the transgression of class divisions. The French myths of the "kept woman," of the attractiveness of the *midinette* (a big-city shopgirl or office clerk, who is supposed to be very sentimental), of the seductive powers of "P'tit Louis" (a "hunk," a good dancer, from the working class), and the innumerable seducers of both sexes in French novels, songs, and films are sufficient proof.

The interest of a parallel such as the one I have just established is that it shows how astonishingly similar meanings can be expressed in areas which seem to be completely unrelated. Yet the greatest attraction of cultural analysis, for me, is the possibility of replacing a dull exchange of invectives with an exploration that is, at the very least, fascinating—a true feast to which I hereby invite you.

Another source of misunderstanding between the French and Americans which should be explored at greater length is their attitudes with respect to various social engagements. Many French people who frequently visit the United States feel "trapped" by American invitations made weeks in advance and as a result do not feel obliged to do what they had agreed to do, back when "they had nothing else planned for that day." A French woman was shocked by the fact that her American colleagues, who had organized a large party in her honor "weeks in advance," were "not at all pleased" when she called the evening of the reception to tell them that she and her companion couldn't come "because they had tickets for a concert which was not to be missed." The couple in question is a sophisticated couple, and very "up" on social conventions in France. They simply had a hard time understanding how others could ask them to commit themselves, long before they could "be sure of being free," and then get angry at their canceling under such circumstances.

An appointment is made. The French person does not show up, does not call, does not apologize, and when later asked why he or she missed the appointment, responds with astonishment, "Oh, I forgot," or "I didn't think it was important," or "I wasn't in the mood," or "I was talking to a friend and I didn't notice the time pass," explanations which he or she takes to be sufficient but which the American will interpret as an insult ("You are not important to me") or as a sign of irresponsibility ("You can never count on them").

The inverse is also common. An American told me with great surprise that her "French sister" (in a family with whom she had spent some time in France) had stopped writing to her after an exchange of letters, which she took to be the cause of this silence that she could not understand. Her "sister" had written that she would be visiting her during a trip to the United States, to which the American had responded with great enthusiasm; then, in the meantime, her uncle became gravely ill. She wrote to her "French sister" and told her, "in all frankness," that because of these family circumstances, her visit would be "inconvenient." This was followed by silence on the part of the "French sister," which the American found incomprehensible. In my notes I have several cases which fall into this category.

It seems clear that in order to understand these misunderstandings, it is the meaning of obligation, of "commitment," and the manner in which it is expressed in each culture that must be researched. It is more than likely that the two meanings do not coincide.

As we see, the analysis of our respective "verities" is only just beginning.

I would like, now, to pause a moment to discuss some of the questions which were asked of me, or which one could ask of me, concerning my cultural analyses.

Supposing that I become aware of my "invisible verities" and that I recognize the existence, and even the validity, of the other's "verities," does this prevent me from being annoyed by this difference, by this "incongruous" behavior? Supposing that I understand that my affective or interrelational needs are informed by my culture, does this diminish their importance? Must I deny these needs?

I cannot sufficiently emphasize the importance of these questions. The issue is not one of power ("which culture will win") but of identity. We have believed for too long that the best quality is adaptability, repeated for too long that in Rome one should do as the Romans. Thanks to my research, I have become very familiar with a most distressing intercultural situation, that of intercultural families in which the difference has been successfully denied. Let me explain. An American woman who has been living in France for twenty years, whose husband is French, "as well as her children," who speaks French fluently and with almost no accent, told me she had done everything possible to adapt. She had succeeded so well that her French family and friends never noticed the price she had had to pay and now feel betrayed by her "sudden need" to hear English spoken, and to return to the United States alone from time to time. The violence with which she described all the "faults" (according to her) of the French, her sense of being trapped in an intolerable contradiction ("Can I tell my own children that their country is insufferable?") revealed a great deal about the price she had paid—and was still paying—for her "success," the adaptation which had wound up making her difference trivial if not invisible. Desperate, she even went to see a psychiatrist, knowing full well that though she was suffering, she "wasn't sick," that there was "nothing wrong" with her.

A Frenchman from a Jewish family "which had lived in France for centuries" and belonged to the *grande bourgeoisie* "never forgave France" for having forced his family to emigrate to the United States during the Second World War. He changed his first name to the American spelling, married an American, gave American names to his children who were "brought up American-style," and refused to speak French. The cultural turmoil is apparent only in the fact that he teaches French literature, with a certain success, so it is said.

Another Frenchman came to the United States for one year and ended up staying ten. He speaks English perfectly, wrote a dissertation on English literature, has American friends, sexual relations with Americans, an American professional life, and takes essentially American-style trips. For several years he has been suffering from depression and mysterious physiological problems and has been treated by a psychiatrist without much success.

Numerous cases on both sides of the Atlantic tell the same story. Anthropologists are quite familiar with this illness; they often begin by succumbing to the temptation of identifying completely with the society they study and of blending into the landscape ("going native"). What saves anthropologists is that they recover quickly, because one cannot discover the identity of the other without being aware of one's own identity. The disturbing number of what I call "cultural casualties" convinced me that it is urgent that we form a new discipline, create a new sort of counselor, the "culturanalyst," who would specialize in intercultural problems. This responsibility rests with anthropology.

Far more numerous are those who, in a way, do not adapt, or who adapt without losing their cultural identity and retain (often unconsciously) certain signs which make their difference apparent: an accent, a way of dressing, a mode of interaction, and so on. Yet these people are not protected from irritation, fatigue, annoyance, intercultural misunderstandings. Adopting a very understandable technique of self-defense, they put together a definite, stereotypical portrait of the French or the Americans, attributing qualities and faults to them, as if these characteristics were inherent in "the foreigner" (among whom they came to live), rather than an artifact of—and a comment on—their own culture. French and Americans have the same attitude also with respect to the other, to the foreigner who comes to settle in or visit their country, and are unavoidably disturbed by the implicit questions posed by difference.

It is the natives who feel that they have the most right to ask: "Why do we need cultural analysis? Let them adapt or leave. Why should I change?"

Because today, cultural differences are impossible to avoid. They are woven into the fabric of our daily lives, and those who do not see this simply have their eyes closed and want to keep them closed at the risk of doing themselves harm. Because cultural differences are here to stay.

Because practicing cultural analysis will in no way change the aspects of myself which I consider to be essential but will enrich me with a new way of thinking, will provide me with an additional tool for my apprehension of the mysterious world around me, will give me access to a new type of pleasure, will afford me interesting discoveries both about myself and the other, both about my culture and that of others. Because I will be able to recognize with humor (and a certain sense of power) situations, phrases, modes of conduct, words which formerly wounded me, bothered me, riled me up or angered me, and which sometimes brought me to despair.

Because I will no longer be afraid of the foreign, of the opaque, of the unknown, of that which is different.

Because rereading the great masters of "my" literature through this lens will give them new meaning, will create bonds which may transcend time and space. Because I will learn to "read" cultural difference in writing, in the structure of a book (even in the place of the table of contents), in the way a chapter is arranged, in the order of a discourse, the persuasiveness of an argument, the definition of "logical."

Because I will have found the source of energy in disjunction, because I will have understood how the gap does not have to be a break but can be rather an inexhaustible source of wonder, an enchanted grotto. Because I will have discovered that there lies the secret of the great artists of today.

Because I know the advantage and the pleasure of speaking more than one language, and because I can imagine the advantage and the pleasure of speaking more than one culture.

Because I can explore what attracts me in the exotic without destroying this atraction. Because I will be able to see the invisible, the exotic in me.

Simply because. For the beauty of the adventure.

Another question often raised is that of cultural change. Our society—every society—is constantly changing and cannot survive without change. How can we perform cultural analysis, which is based on the constancy of certain premises, in a society in perpetual flux?

My answer, here again, will be controversial. I am not offering it as a truth, but as food for thought. The many polls of all kinds, taken every day on every topic, have put us in the habit of thinking that when certain statistics change, our society changes as well. I will not expand on this topic; there is nothing new in what I am saying. Sociologists and anthropologists who have studied "cultural change" have contributed vastly to reinforcing our conviction that social change and cultural change are identical; this, I maintain, is a serious mistake. To be persuaded, one need only consider for a moment the recent "revolutions" of the western world: the sexual revolution, May '68 in France or "the sixties" in the United States, the ecological revolution, feminism, the "new breed of fathers," and so on. One cannot deny that change has occurred. But on further study, it quickly becomes apparent that each of these revolutions happened in a different way, according to the culture of the revolutionaries. The incomprehension of French feminism by American feminists is equaled only by the incomprehension of American feminism by French feminists. The same is true of other revolutions. In surveying young people of both countries, I was surprised to find, time and again, the same deep-seated attitudes as those of their parents and grandparents, but accompanied by a call for international tolerance and expressed in the vocabulary of the young.

Moreover, one need not be especially perceptive to note that our young people resemble each other more than they resemble their parents, that our skyscrapers resemble each other, our supermarkets resemble each other, our restaurants resemble each other, our cars resemble each other; that Americans buy their French bread, croissants, Perrier, cheeses, mustard, and wines, just as the French buy their American Coca-Cola, bourbon, ketchup, jeans, hamburgers, television shows, films, records, and so on. On both sides of the Atlantic, newspaper articles denounce the "invasion" of the other culture or of the other language, laugh about the snobbery of such and such a trend, such and such a "foreign" drink; we find the same cries of alarm, the same barriers erected. There are the same problems and worries concerning crime, lack of security, drug traffic, teenage suicide, "moral decadence," the solitude of the aged, the scandal of poverty; the nuclear threat, cancer, heart attacks, divorce, alienation, stress; alcoholism; violence. . . . More than one traveler, in one direction or the other, has been surprised at not being surprised, disappointed to find the familiar when he was expecting the shock of the foreign.

Every day, technological revolutions seem to accelerate this race toward uniformity. How can such changes, common to both our societies—visible, undeniable changes—be compatible with the idea of our profound cultural differences?

A distinction must be made between changes that are real, but which I would call "surface" changes, and the resistance of cultural premises to change. And I insist here on the fact that "surface" does not mean "superficial." These changes are not at all illusory, are not the result of mistaken perceptions or defective research. Though these changes are on the "surface," they are no less important. The mistake is not in believing that they exist; it consists instead in making them the proof, the unquestionable sign of cultural change.

It is easier to distinguish between these two types of changes if we take the transformation of language as an example. At a level which corresponds to what I call the "surface," changes are obvious and undeniable, even in the space of twenty years, as the (at times discouraged) teachers of both countries can attest. One need only live a life of normal length to witness syntactical changes (or at least strong pressures on syntax to change) as well as, and especially, changes in vocabulary. These changes are not great enough, however, to prevent us from understanding texts written long before (sometimes very long before) our birth. A time comes when understanding becomes more and more difficult, and if we go back far enough, reading becomes impossible without some training. This is the case for Old French, for example. Yet it is easier for me to learn to read (and understand) Old French in school if I am French than it is to learn a completely foreign language.

Just as they do in language, profound, irreversible cultural changes take place very slowly; opposed to these are what I would call "social" changes—changes we not only can witness, but the nature and process of which we can also study and analyze.

If I cannot become conscious of cultural change, it is because such an act would be, by its very nature, contradictory. That which is evident exists or does not exist; it does not transform itself before my eyes. What is more, if by definition my cultural premises inform my way of apprehending the world, my "truth," they are invisible to me, I am not aware of them. Through the effort of analysis I can become aware of their existence and maybe even discover the form that some of them take, but I cannot, no matter how hard I try, become aware of their transformation, because it is precisely in this case that I would not recognize them. My cultural premises cannot both be mine and be opaque. On the contrary, they are defined by their transparency.

In other words, cultural premises do not change; they die, or, rather, they rejoin other premises in premise paradise, between cultural reincarnations. And as our premises are innumerable, the retirement of one and recombination of others go unnoticed. The phenomenon of cultural change can therefore only be apprehended in retrospect, long, long after it has taken place, when the invisible, the transparent, has become opaque. It then pertains to a kind of cultural archaeology.

When there is change of the type that I call "social," or "surface," cultural premises do not change; they remain the same, but the form by which they are expressed changes. It is, so to speak, the cultural "vocabulary" that changes. It is only from this perspective that we can understand how change and continuity coexist in every society, how people of different "classes," city dwellers and country people, young and old—in short, people who are apparently (that is to say "in appearance," "on the surface") different—can belong to and reproduce the same culture, share the same cultural premises, the truth of which they constantly reaffirm unknowingly and the continuity of which they assure through all their contacts with those younger than they. And, I repeat, since these premises coexist, no matter what their number and contradictory nature, the way in which I express them will be unique to me, which explains how I can be a cultural being and preserve my individuality, not be a robot. In other words, I have the same sort of relationship with my culture as with my native tongue: I use the same syntax and vocabulary as do thousands or millions of other people. Some of our expressions are very similar, or even identical (clichés, polite formulas, etc.), but most of the phrases we create every day within this common language are unique, bear our own stamp and that of the context in which we create them.

Like language, culture that does not change becomes fixed and dies. But also like language, culture changes at a rhythm that transcends the length of human life. And if the change is very great, the culture no longer exists as such but becomes another culture. The two cultures then have similarities which can be recognized through analysis, but they have become opaque to one another, as is the case with languages like French and Latin, for example.

Such a theory has numerous implications, which cannot help but create ripples, if not waves. One of these implications is that wanting to "preserve" a culture is an idea destined to fail. Indeed, I carry my own culture, but I cannot transmit it without the contribution of those who share my culture, without the communication network that gives meaning to my exchanges. This means that in order to live and persist, a culture must be reaffirmed and renewed through a constant churning which is out of my control, which does not depend on my will, insofar as I myself particpate in this churning without being conscious of it. My culture is in me, is me, but transcends me. If it does not transcend me, it does not exist. I can only transmit my "truth" unconsciously, by living it involuntarily. As soon as I recognize it as "my" truth, I also recognize its arbitrary nature and can no longer affirm its unquestionable value, since I am now aware that it is not unique (it is no longer "the" truth). In order to preserve, I must identify and define, I must limit and circumscribe. In so doing, whether I like it or not, I posit that what I want to preserve is outside of myself. Thus, if I cut off my hand, I can preserve it in formaldehyde, but it no longer lives, whereas I can live without it. In order for it to continue to live, it must be grafted onto another living body, in which case it will no longer be my hand. For my hand to remain my hand, it must be part of the system I call my body, must participate in the life of this body which gives it life. Detached from me, it can be "preserved" and dead, or live and no longer be mine, and therefore no longer be itself. Can we still say that it is "a hand," if it is grafted onto a living system other than a human body, which does not reject it but transforms its use and meaning? (This possibility is not just science fiction.) The same is true, in a sense, for my culture. This is why any effort to "preserve" a culture is a contradiction in terms (and therefore destined to fail). We can only preserve traditions, customs, types of music, dishes, and so on—in short, a "vocabulary" from our past. (All that we call "civilization" therefore depends on this preservation effort and should not be confused with culture, in the anthropological sense of the word.)

Consequently, no matter how they try, immigrants cannot prevent their children from becoming cultural products of the adopted country. Through their efforts at preservation, they can only accentuate the gap between the two cultures and prevent harmonization. They will succeed in making the split painful, but in no way can they prevent cultural crossbreeding. There is not, and there never really has been, a "pure culture" (even in minuscule isolated atolls like Nukuoro, there has always been intercultural contact). The difficulty for the immigrant, whatever his or her social class, arises from the difficulty of not becoming entirely "invisible" by adapting completely while, at the same time, not becoming "too visible" by declining to adapt. This choice, which because of its contextual nature is in a constant state of flux, will determine the way in which his or her children will experience their biculturalism (as an asset or a hindrance).

Of course, I am speaking here of individual immigration, not of mass immigration, which does not allow one to escape acculturation (supposing one would like to) but which can slow the process. It seems that, in all cases, acculturation is complete in two generations. The situation of black Americans presents a special case. Inasmuch as there was not immigration but importation, slavery, and that acculturation was forbidden and resulted in harm (and often death), much more than the suppression of slavery was necessary for blacks to live openly the conflict of their double cultural belonging. Within the United States, blacks may accentuate their belonging to the black culture in order to distinguish themselves from whites and refuse to blend in. But when a black American recounts his travels in France, Spain, or Africa, there is no mistaking it, an American is speaking. And it is not just a matter of the "privileged" class which has the means to travel, since the army is one of the best travel agents.

In another connection, I am persuaded that the American "black culture" constitutes a type of hyphen between French and American cultures and that certain misunderstandings between American blacks and whites closely resemble Franco-American misunderstandings. The conversation, the word games, the lively teasing, the punctuating laughter of black Americans seem very close to those of the French. The same is true of certain parent-child relationships, and of relationships in the couple. The more I inquire among black Americans, the more I read of their literature, oral poetry, and ethnographies, the more I am convinced that these areas of resemblance exist. But I made this discovery rather late in my research. I was therefore unable to establish whether or not these resemblances would provide sufficient grounds for asserting a (relative) lack of intercultural misunderstandings between black Americans and the French.

If my culture, which lives in me and by me, does not depend on my existence (in no way will my culture be touched, weakened, or endangered when I die), this means that it does not belong to me any more than it does to any other; that I cannot pretend to be a better representative of it than anyone else, to be its privileged trustee. Despite all my possible illusions on this subject, I cannot be "more French" than X or Y, whether my ancestors were Gauls, Celts, Latins, or Algerians. But the fact that I think in terms of having a greater or lesser right to cultural belonging is one of my "invisible verities," one of my French "truths," which I share as much with the previously acculturated as with the recently acculturated. A culture is a way of seeing the world, not a right of prior membership.

I need not insist on the consequences of such an affirmation.

Another question which often arises in relation to cultural analysis is that of "regional differences." We all know that there are great differences between the northern and southern United States, between Brittany and the Midi of France, and so on. What should we make of these differences? How can we reconcile these differences with the idea of culture?

Here again, as in the case of "social changes" mentioned earlier, it is a matter of surface differences—real differences, but on another level from that of meaning. The difference is in the manner of expression, not in the meaning of that which is expressed. Cultural premises live in the rarefied world of the abstract, of logic; regional differences, social changes, belong, on the other hand, to the concrete world of representation. The multiplicity of representations is what makes cultural analysis difficult but fascinating. The challenge consists in uncovering how "texts" which belong to the same culture but which appear to be different (entering a house and having a conversation, for example) can affirm the same truth, can be two equally valid expressions of the same cultural proposition; or else how "texts" which belong to different cultures, but which we suppose to be identical in the name of the universality of human sentiments (friendship, love, family, etc.), can express different cultural propositions and even affirm contrary truths (hence the possibility of intercultural misunderstandings).

For instance, I outlined earlier how the significance of money for Americans and that of seduction for the French could become less opaque if seen side by side. If we presuppose that money (or seduction) has the same significance in the two cultures, we run into misunderstandings. Let us, for an instant, consider the unsaid, implicit meaning of money for the French.

In her book *La Mémoire Longue*, Françoise Zonabend extensively analyzes the nature and function of certain exchanges (gifts, food, services, knowledge, verbal exchanges) in the community of Minot and shows how exchanges "create the cohesion of kin groups, and the solidarity of the neighborhood." She also shows how "people are reluctant to use money for products that can be obtained otherwise" and how "these exchanges express and reaffirm the ties among households." This bookkeeping method of exchanges (the interruption of which would signify a rupture, a refusal to maintain ties) over time constitutes, roughly, what she calls "long-term memory." From this perspective, money, with which exchanges are immediately settled, would constitute not even "short-term memory" but the absence of memory, a kind of degree zero of relations.*

We now remember how, in the chapter on conversation, the absence of a relationship between the French customer and shopkeeper (the baker, for example) was apparent in that their verbal exchange was kept to an absolute minimum: I ask for bread, receive the bread, pay, leave with "my" bread; the bread is exchanged for money, the transaction is completed. Conversation allows us to transform an exchange without money into an exchange with memory and a necessary act (buying, selling) into a social act. In fact, one guiding thread becomes clear from all the analyses in the preceding chapters: what seems the most opaque to Americans are the different ways in which the French affirm or reaffirm bonds, in which they separate those in the group from those outside the group, in which they "tell" the other that he or she is or is not part of the group. My social "debts" situate me in a network, my financial debts do not. And this has nothing to do with the "moral" or "immoral" value of money: money is simply "foreign" to the relational system that holds meaning for the French.

In Nukuoro, as we needed help and services of all kinds, we hired or made agreements with several people on the island and paid for these services with money, since we had neither land, nor coconut groves, nor taro—in short, neither objects nor talents which would allow us to enter into the system of local exchange. The people of Nukuoro recognized our "destitute" condition, measured on the local scale, and could use this money to purchase imported objects. This is why they agreed to be paid for the fish they caught for us, or for the

*The English edition of *La Mémoire Longue* is *The Enduring Memory*, trans. Anthony Forster (Wolfeboro, N.H.: The Longwood Publishing Group, 1985).

services for which we were totally at their mercy. Yet we soon discovered that the money we gave them in no way freed us from the kinship obligations which defined the networks into which we had been integrated and without which no one would have "helped" us. As the Nukuoro were not in the habit of using money, other than to buy what "the ship" brought every two or even three months (rice, batteries and flashlights, printed cotton, cigarettes, and other such objects), they did not hesitate, in the name of our kinship ties, to ask us to order for them, or to bring back from our trips to the United States, the most unexpected items (gold wedding rings, musical instruments, etc.). They did not do this to benefit from our naïveté or out of greed but because only "gifts" (whatever they were, regardless of their price, and hence their sometimes "extravagant," sometimes "insignificant" value in our eyes) could allow us to participate in a system of exchanges which had meaning for them and in which money played absolutely no part.

Industrialization, urbanization, modernization, and all other words ending in -ion, have rendered exchanges like those of Minot, or of Nukuoro, extremely difficult but have in no way diminished their meaning and importance for the French. There has, therefore, been "social" change, but not "cultural" change. The cultural premise which might take the form "I exist in a network" molds my French way of seeing just as much, whether I (French) live in Paris or in a tiny little village in the middle of nowhere, whether I write *l'enfer, c'est les autres*, ("hell is others") or *Essai sur le don (The Gift)*. What changes is my way of expressing this truth, not the truth itself.

Similarly, an American cultural premise, which is expressed in several ways, can be seen in the analyses of the preceding chapters. This premise could take the following form: "I exist outside all networks." This does not mean that these networks do not exist or that they have no importance for me (an American), but that I make myself, I define myself. Whoever I am in American society, wherever I come from, whatever I have, I create the fabric of my identity, as is evoked, in a more limited context, by the expression "self-made man."

In French culture then, I am always a product of the networks that give me my identity (hence the little social game that consists of uncovering someone's "origins") and provide the source of my energy. Consequently, whatever the identity I assert, it can be questioned by anyone from the same network (in the extreme, by anyone of French culture), and very often this is what happens; my "true" identity is always given to me by others. My French identity, therefore, will always be conferred by the other, the "true Frenchman or French woman" whose French identity will in turn be defined by others. Hence Sartre's famous *l'enfer, c'est les autres*. But, if the others were always and only hell, such a system could not survive but would rapidly head for destruction.

The others, in French culture, are also "paradise": I am as much fed, carried, made significant by the network of relationships which defines me as I can be trapped, stifled, and oppressed by it. Without this network, I am out of my element, and I suffer all the more as I am not conscious of this.

On the contrary, if I tell Americans that I am an "American," they may express surprise, but they will not question my assertion, no matter what type of accent I have. They may ask me where I am from, but, here again, they do not do this in order to expose my dissimulation (unless there is an issue of illegal immigration). It is not because Americans are more generous or less skeptical than the French but essentially because it is my business if I want to define myself in this way, and other peoples' efforts to make me to otherwise will not change anything. A recent American expression is interesting in this respect: lately we have heard a great deal about "new Americans," a term which designates those who have immigrated recently and who may not even speak English yet. The expression is in no way pejorative; on the contrary, it underscores one's right to this new identity.

Because I am responsible for my identity, I have no reason to hide my "origins," since they do not define me. (If my origins are quite humble, I can only be proud of my success; if I come from high society, I must prove I can stay there, and if I fall from it, I am responsible for my fall.) This explains why Americans are not embarrassed by questions that French people would find "personal" ("What do your parents do?") and why the biographies of people in the public eye are never secret. That the father or brother of a president is, or was, an alcoholic or a good-for-nothing has no bearing whatsoever.

As an American, therefore, I can go from one network to another, try them all and reject them, I can defy everyone's opinions. I have learned that I am, and always will be, my only judge. I am therefore responsible for my own happiness; hence my anguish. I also carry my own hell within myself.

To conclude and close the circle (my French culture is showing through), I would like to return to the turtles which, once cultural analysis has begun, are infinite: this book, which I finish with these lines, is itself a cultural text to be analyzed. I know that if I researched, compared, and sought to understand, it was no accident.